THE CHRISTIAN COUNSELOR'S CASEBOOK

By
Jay E. Adams

A Workbook
designed for individual or class use
in conjunction with
Competent to Counsel
and
The Christian Counselor's Manual

PRESBYTERIAN AND REFORMED PUBLISHING COMPANY
Phillipsburg, New Jersey 08865

First printing, May 1974
Second printing, January 1975
Third printing, December 1976
Fourth printing, September 1977
Fifth printing, May 1979
Sixth printing, February 1981
Seventh printing, February 1982
Eighth printing, December 1984

Library of Congress Catalog Card Number 74-81707
Printed in the United States of America

INTRODUCTION

This counseling casebook is designed for the classroom, the study, or ministerial seminars.[1] The *Casebook* may be used as a companion volume to *Competent to Counsel* and *The Christian Counselor's Manual*.[2] It is a workbook; answers to the problem questions following each case will be found in these books.

Cases are based upon actual counseling experiences, but all cases have been altered to make them utterly unidentifiable. Some are composites; most have been simplified to stress particular issues and problems. Frequently they appear as slices or snapshots rather than as wholes or moving pictures. The cases have been selected representatively to cover the sorts of problems most frequently encountered in the course of ordinary pastoral counseling. Moreover, they have been written and are presented in a manner calculated to introduce the student to as many biblical solutions and methods and biblically based procedures as possible. These are all fully described in the *Manual*.

The cases usually stress more than one counseling practice, but even those that focus more directly upon one are developed in ways that attempt to open up possibilities for the discussion of others. This is true particularly since there is no one correct answer to some of the

---

1. Three or four ministers (or the members of a ministerium) may meet regularly over a period of time to discuss representative cases. At each seminar, each minister should be prepared to present a case together with his understanding of and suggestions for handling the problem(s) involved. His conclusions should be substantiated by marginal references. In the classroom, or in the ministerium, it is possible to present cases by role playing them.
2. Jay E. Adams, *The Christian Counselor's Manual* (Nutley, N. J.: Presbyterian and Reformed Publishing Co., 1973). Answers to the problem questions could have been included in this volume, but the decision to point to the *Manual*, and to provide space for references, was made because the instructional values of such study and research seemed much greater. Moreover, this approach seemed less likely to encourage "pat" answers and seemed rather to lead to thinking through all aspects of the problems involved in each case.

problem questions that follow the cases. Depending upon details not given in the *Casebook*[3] (and the reader should remember that many factors converge in every counseling case that give to it particular qualities and dimensions that distinguish it from others), a counselor may find that he must choose from among various possibilities. Hopefully, choosing will help to make him think more broadly and tentatively until all of the pertinent facts are in.

In actual counseling situations nonverbal as well as verbal feedback helps the counselor and may encourage (or discourage) the direction that his thrusts will take (e.g., he may determine to use intensive rather than extensive questioning[4]). The idea behind the questions that are appended to the cases, then, is to raise important and pertinent issues (though not exhaustively) that the counselor ought to have in mind, together with some of the biblical approaches and the solutions that in facing a similar case might be considered by a counselor.

Blanks left for composing homework assignments ought not be passed over since the ability to give and to *write* concrete directions growing out of and consistent with biblical principles and methods is vital to scriptural counseling.

There are only two sections in the *Casebook*: (1) Opening Sessions; (2) Sessions in Process. Beyond this basic division, cases have been presented randomly with no attempt to classify them according to the nature of problems. This was done in order to enable the student to face each case as he will in actual counseling. Obviously, the cases will appear randomly in real life with no clues growing out of artificial classification. Thus, as in the counseling room, the *Casebook* forces him to learn to identify the problem in each case on the basis of its own characteristics.

There are three major purposes in view:

(1) To provide practice in learning how to identify various sorts of problems according to biblical norms.
(2) To provide practice in laying out biblical plans of action for dealing with these problems.
(3) To provide familiarity with a wide variety of representative types of problems that every counselor sooner or later may encounter.

---

3. These may be supplied in presenting the case.
4. Cf. *The Christian Counselor's Manual*, pp. 252-256.

The *Casebook* layout as a workbook provides space (1) for answers to problem questions, (2) for written homework assignments, and (3) for marginal references. References to the Scriptures, to the *Manual,* and to other works, together with interpretive annotations, can be entered into the margins. A superscript numeral at the end of a sentence in the text will easily indicate that marginal entry to which it refers. Cross references to other cases in the book, or to other homework assignments or answers to problems, also may be entered. By rereading the *Casebook* from time to time, one may get help from paradigm cases, assignments, plans, etc., and if he continues to make notations and entries in the *Casebook* from time to time, at length he will have a valuable, personalized reference volume.[5]

In conclusion, I must express deep gratitude to Howard Eyrick, Chet Lanious, Ron Lutz, and John Wall for their invaluable assistance in the preparation of this volume. Also to Mr. Don Worch let me say "thanks" for making the early publication of this book possible.

---

5. Paradigm cases also may be noted in their proper places in the space provided in the *Manual,* pp. 453-456.

SAMPLE CASE

Bob, a former seminary classmate, now pastor of a conservative church in a neighboring town, has made a lunch date with you. You are startled that he is here, as he puts it, "to discuss some serious doubts concerning the basic doctrines of Christianity."

"I don't understand exactly why," he continues, "but I seem to be losing my grip on everything I used to believe firmly, everything I used to hold dear."

You remember Bob as a staunch defender of the faith. You suspect that the problems may be complex. Wondering whether other than intellectual doubts may be part of the picture, you probe to find out how the work of the church has been progressing.

"These doubts have been so disturbing I haven't been able to do my work well—I'm behind in everything. I've been so depressed over doubt I've been getting further behind each week. I can barely stay ahead with my sermon preparation, I haven't made a visit for weeks, and to top it off I have announced a special series of messages on the Christian family, beginning next month, that I can't get going on. I'm ready to give up."

"When did you begin to get behind?"

"About two months ago."

"When did your doubts begin?"

Bob's glum look slowly changed to a thoughtful frown: "I remember; I had a wedding and a funeral and four serious counseling cases all in the same week. I got behind on everything because of these events. Soon after, I remember having to

Which is the chicken; which the egg?

Cf. C. to C., p. 116

Here is where it began; should have never given in to feelings.
Cf. II Cor. 4:8-9
(down, but not out)

prepare a sermon on the inspiration of the Scriptures. But because I was so rushed, I did a very superficial job. I remember thinking, 'If I can't think or speak clearly or convincingly about this doctrine maybe I don't believe it myself.' I had to keep preaching, but my heart wasn't in it."

"How about your regular schedule, Bob? For the family, study, worship, etc.? Are you working all day long? Are you trying to catch up?"

Attempt to escape; find quick satisfaction

Bob slumped deeper into his seat. "Think! I'm going to speak about the family next month; and I'm a failure myself. I've neglected everything—including my family. I've been sitting brooding rather than working. I even watched a soap opera on TV the other morning, in my study."

What is the TV doing there?

Problems:

1. What do you suspect Bob's problem is?

   Depression as the result of allowing responsibilities to pile up following a week of getting behind legitimately. His doubts probably are about himself rather than about God.

2. What would you advise Bob?

   To shelve his questions and doubts temporarily (I'd tell him that he is in no condition to make a good judgment about them) and to catch up on his responsibilities (then, and only then, can the doubts -- if they still remain -- be considered rightly). Cf. *Manual*, p. 428; pp. 375-380. (esp. pp. 379, 380)

3. Would you set up formal counseling with Bob?

   Not unless he asked for it, or if he did not think he could do the homework. Note follow up on homework assmnt #6.

Homework

1. Make list of visits to be made in order of priority—schedule these + — make crucial visits NO MATTER HOW YOU FEEL!

2. Take out a series of old sermons and preach these for the next three or four weeks while you concentrate on the new series. WRITE OUT SOMETHING EACH DAY REGARDLESS.

3. Ask God's forgiveness for all, and seek His help.

4. Remove TV from study!

5. Schedule time for all necessary activities.

6. Lets have lunch again when you are caught up if you still have doubts.

PART ONE
OPENING SESSIONS

"THE PISTOL IS AT MY HEAD"

Your telephone rings one morning at one o'clock, and you find yourself speaking with Mary, a middle-aged married woman, the mother of two teenagers, who, together with her family, is a member of your congregation: You have noticed that she has missed services recently, but you had no other indication of any difficulty. However, there is no doubt in your mind as you listen to her now that she has been drinking heavily, and worse yet, she is threatening to commit suicide. You talk, trying to get the story. Her response to your questions about how she expects to take her life is both swift and frightening: "The pistol is at my head as I speak." You urge Mary to talk over her problem, assuring her that the situation indeed is serious and should get immediate attention. But, she refuses to tell you anything more unless you swear never to reveal to anyone what she tells you.

Problems:

1. Should you accept this condition? Justify your answer biblically.

2. Is there any other way of handling the problem?

3. What would be your goals and methods in meeting the threat of suicide?

Homework

"NOTHING LEFT" TO THEIR MARRIAGE

"There is nothing left to our marriage. . . ." That's the way Milton put it as he ended a long tale of disagreement, heartache, and frustration. To which he added (as the final fillip): "I don't have a speck of love left for Marge any more." She was quick to agree: ". . . And I don't love him either; all of the feeling I once had for Milt has drained out." They had come not for help but to obtain salve for their sore consciences. As Christians, they knew they had no biblical grounds for the divorce which they were contemplating. Yet, in disobedience to God's Word they were intent upon getting it because life together any longer seemed unbearable. "Perhaps if we explain our situation to a Christian counselor, he will agree with us and reassure us that in our case a divorce is warranted; that God will make an exception." That was the way they thought. They are here not to seek reconciliation, but rather to obtain balm from Gilead to rub on their guilty consciences.

Problems:

1. What erroneous notion do Milton and Marge hold in common?

2. What do they need?

3. How will you meet this need?

Homework

5

SHE SIMPLY HAD BEEN WAITING

Eight days after Christmas Phyllis announced to Frank, "I'm leaving you; I waited to tell you so that I wouldn't spoil your holiday." The announcement struck him like lightning out of the blue. Until that very moment he had thought that they had an ideal marriage. He thought— "They rarely argued; he was easy going and asked little more of her than to make the meals, wash the clothes, and keep house. He didn't run around—every night in the week you could find him at home domestically reading the newspaper or watching TV. They were both Christians; went to church regularly. He loved her deeply, they had raised three children successfully (after all, Franklin Jr. had just left home for his second semester at Christian University, and Betty and Joan were already married to Christian husbands and had begun to raise their families). What could have gotten into Phyllis?" he asked himself in startled disbelief. But Phyllis wouldn't talk about it, and said that she wouldn't go with him for help. Now, here he sits alone in your study pleading: "Pastor, help me; I don't want to lose Phyllis. I love her! What happened? Where did things go wrong?"

Problems:

1. What do you think may be behind Phyllis' decision?

2. How firm do you think her decision is?

3. What must you do—immediately? ultimately?

4. Against what dangers must you guard?

Homework

THE JOB HUNTER

"We owe everyone in town, and if Warren doesn't soon get a good job and keep it we may be tarred and feathered and run out of town!" That was the icing that Florence put on the cake. Warren, quite honestly, had detailed a thirteen-year history of failure to make good at supporting his family of three (they had two children—Sally and Rose). Time and again they had been bailed out of financial ruin by Florence's father, but the last time he had put his foot down. "Never again!" he roared. "If you don't make it this time, you can sink!" That was six months ago. At the time everything had looked rosy. Both had become Christians; for a while Warren's new job as head of the shipping department in a large printing firm looked secure, he enjoyed it, and he seemed well suited for the work. But gradually the old problem had returned. Disagreements, complaints, anger, and resentment toward his employer and fellow workers grew until two days ago in a fiery exchange with the plant manager he stormed out of the place and quit. It was then that Florence had insisted upon coming to you for help.

Problems:

1. What problems are apparent?

2. What other problems might possibly be present?

3. Would it be of importance to explore the content of the argument? Why?

4. What patterns may exist?

Homework

"I HEARD GOD'S VOICE TELLING ME TO GO TO AFRICA"

"You say that they had you arrested when you tried to force your way on to an airliner heading for Africa?" "Yes—and I'm going to get there yet! I know I was wrong in trying to serve God as I did. I now know that I should have earned the money for my ticket instead of acting so impulsively upon His call. But God has called me to Africa. I know that. I heard His voice as clearly as I hear yours right now. And this was after three days of continuous earnest prayer to discover what God wanted me to do with my life. Surely then, it could not have been of the devil." Twenty-three-year-old Richard, a seminary student, who had never acted erratically before, who was a fine student, and who seemed doctrinally sound, suddenly raced out of his room, hailing a taxi to the airport. Fleeing from the taxi without paying the cabbie, he escaped into the crowd, only to be arrested when insisting that he be allowed to board—without a ticket—a Florida-bound plane that he claimed was headed for Africa.

Problems:

1. To what could Rick's problem be attributed?

2. What line of questioning would you pursue to discover the facts behind his bizarre behavior?

3. How would you deal with his behavior?

Homework

GUIDANCE — OR MORE?

"Here on the pink sheet you list your problem as 'church membership,' Mike," says the counselor. "Would you explain what you mean by that?"

"Sure. Here's the situation. I am single, 25 years old, and attend two churches. I like both of them very much, but I know that I should become a member at one and devote all of my energies there. So I've been praying for guidance for a long time, but the Lord still hasn't shown me which church I should join. What do you think I should do?"

"Well, what have you done to discover the Lord's will in this matter?"

"I've mostly prayed a lot that He would show me. I really believe He will."

"That's fine, but how have you been expecting Him to reveal His will to you?"

"Well, the normal ways, I suppose. You know, by little signs and feelings. I want to really know inside where I should be, and have a real peace about it."

Problems:

1. Would you consider this a crisis situation or rather an opportunity for educational counseling?

2. Is there a lot more "beneath" Mike's explanation than seems to appear on the surface?

3. How would you find out, if you think so?

4. What is your next step in counseling?

Homework

THE AFFAIR

Sharon and Eric, friends of one of your elders, at his suggestion have come for help in reconciling their marriage. They have been living apart for about one month, ever since Sharon found out about THE AFFAIR.

Eric declares: "She's frigid! What was I supposed to do?" as he openly tells of his subsequent unfaithfulness. There had been no sexual relations for over six months prior to his adultery.

"But don't forget to tell him about those times that you beat me . . . , and when you threatened my life! You were drunk, but I got scared! Billy (our son) won't even stay in the same room with you when you're like that. Everyone is afraid . . . and . . . fear and sex don't mix." Sharon cries.

"Eric, you are going to have to ask Sharon for forgiveness, and Sharon, you will have to forgive him if you expect to put this marriage together again," you counsel. "Moreover, we must discuss the even more basic matter of seeking God's forgiveness in Christ. That's where reconciliation and new life begin."

"I *have* forgiven him, but I can't forget. Forgiveness doesn't demand forgetting, does it? I know that I love Eric, but I don't know whether I ever will be able to give myself to him again. You can't have good sexual relations when you are scared to death!"

Problems:

1. The problems here are numerous and varied. How may they be sorted out? What are they?

2. How may the counselor continue to offer the dual help (in reconciliation and in introducing them to Christ) that he already has begun to hold out?

3. What of Sharon's fear? Should she be counseled to move back?

4. Discuss forgiveness in this case.

Homework

I'VE GOT A SECRET

Violet is now 54 years old. She is a Christian, lives with her son and his wife, and for many years has complained of depression. She does little or nothing else, but does still attend church regularly. Yet every week she comes home more upset and gets more depressed than before.

In this first session she has admitted to bitterness and resentment that she connects vaguely with church attendance. She claims to be lonely, says she daydreams, and on her Personal Data Inventory hints at an undisclosed problem: ". . . and, there is a difficulty that I could mention only to God." Initial inquiries about this matter are met with hesitance, reluctance to speak, evasion, and embarrassment.

Problems:

1. How will you begin?

2. In what area(s) is the undisclosed problem likely to lie?

3. How important will it be to find out what this problem is?

4. In what ways may you encourage her to reveal the problem? Do you think that she wants to disclose it to you?

Homework

LOTS OF PROBLEMS

"Like you said at the beginning, after hearing all of these problems I can see that this is a very complicated situation," says the counselor during his first session with Vic and Marie.

"Right! Putting together two messed up lives like ours, plus the five children from previous marriages, makes for a wild household," says the gloomy 45-year-old husband.

"Yes, I can see why you get frustrated. Now, before you go there's just one more thing I need to know. You mentioned that Paul (your 17-year-old son) and Bill (Marie's 16-year-old) fight constantly, and that you find it difficult to discipline them about it. I suppose that this is one of the biggest sources of irritation in the family. What kinds of things do they fight about?"

"Well, they fight about almost everything," Vic responds quickly. "Who's better in football, who's better in school, who gets away with the most around the house. You know, things like that, *all* the time!"

"There's probably a lot of competitiveness due to their close ages, wouldn't you say?"

"Yes, I'm sure of that."

"O.K., we'll keep that in mind. Well, I think we are starting to get a much better picture now than what we had an hour ago. I hope that this has helped you to understand what the situation is. We'll see you next week at the same time."

Problems:

1. The counselor has missed the boat. How?

2. What did Vic and Marie need in this first session that he failed to give them?

3. How might he have done so without neglecting the concerns that he had?

Homework

SPENDTHRIFT

You requested this session; and Joe, a member of your congregation, has come willingly. Your request grew out of a disturbing response last Sunday that Joe gave to a suggestion that he might consider sending his first and only child to kindergarten at a nearby Christian school. On that occasion Joe had remarked: "I couldn't possibly afford the tuition." Yet you know from the nature of his job as head draftsman in his firm that he is earning a respectable income.

You confront him with your problem and wonder if there is anything else in the picture and offer to help if you can. Joe seizes upon the offer and pours out an amazing story in which he confesses that he has a serious problem with extravagant spending.

He puts it like this: "I want to stop, but before I know it I find myself buying all sorts of unnecessary things. I make inordinate use of credit cards; the grocery bill is always higher whenever I accompany Helen on her shopping trips. It's terrible! I know that, and I'm ashamed. Pastor, what can I do to stop? I've tried many times, but I can't keep my money in my pocket."

You discover that Joe is planning to find a second job to help meet his expenses. Joe knows his wife is worried, but doesn't see any way out.

Problems:

1. What long-range program might be set up?

2. What short term advice might be given?

3. What else would you want to know at this first session?

4. Is it important to include Helen in subsequent sessions? Why?

5. How would you discuss biblical stewardship with Joe?

Homework

WHY BE DEPRESSED?—YOU'RE A CHRISTIAN

"So the main problem you'd like help with is depression," says the counselor. "We'll see what we can do about it, Jim."

"Good, I'm hoping to find some relief soon," responds the college sophomore.

"First of all, Jim, do you know Jesus Christ as your own personal Savior?"

"Yes I do, Sir. I've been a Christian since I was a young child."

"So you've trusted in Him for forgiveness of sins, and you know that God is your Father?"

"Yes, that's right."

"Well then, as a child of God, it's important for you to know and meditate on the promises of God. Have you ever memorized Scripture?"

"I guess I know a lot of familiar verses by heart, but I've never conducted a conscientious program of memorization."

"Well, I'd like you to do just that. Philippians 4:4 says, 'Rejoice in the Lord always, again I say rejoice.' When you start to get depressed remind yourself of this verse. As a Christian you have plenty to be joyful about."

Problems:

1. What do you think of this counselor's approach?

2. If you disagree with his method of dealing with depression, suggest another.

3. The counselor's heart and his concern are right. How can these concerns be maintained but more realistically applied to the counselee's problem?

Homework

"HE MOLESTED OUR DAUGHTER"

I've forgiven him, but how can I ever trust him again? That was the problem, as Shirley presented it. She wanted to try to reconstruct a marriage out of the pieces that had been scattered all over during the last month ever since THE INCIDENT. Brad, her husband, had begged for forgiveness, claiming that he had lost his head after Shirley had refused to have sexual relations with him for three months, and . . . "it only happened then, because our 16-year-old daughter purposely tempted me," he claimed. Shirley's reply to this was: "All the more reason for lack of trust—if he isn't lying then there are two of them that I can't trust!" Their questions: (1) Should Brad return home? and (2) How could she ever trust him in the home? ("I could never go to sleep at night and be sure the children were safe.")

Problems:

1. What will you advise?

2. What of the future safety of the daughter: Can this reasonably be assured? How?

3. What is the particular problem that probably led Brad to make sexual advances toward his daughter?

4. Can trust be reestablished? Should it be? If so, how?

5. What must be done for the daughter?

Homework

LOCK THE DOOR?

Sally, the 38-year-old mother of five children, says that she doesn't know what it means to be saved. (Both she and her husband are Roman Catholics.)

At the present time Paul (her husband) is living with another woman. There are four children at home. (The oldest daughter lives alone. She just recently had an abortion.) Sally admittedly has big problems disciplining the kids.

An area of continual frustration for Sally is her sexual relationship with Paul. Though she gets angry and violently upset whenever he calls or visits the children, she also becomes sexually hungry and allows him to come to her for sex every few weeks. This has been a regular pattern over the past six months. Afterward she feels guilty, confused, and even more angry. She asks, "Should I lock the door?" In addition to anger at her husband, she expresses bitterness toward her parents for their lack of concern for her and her children.

Sally sought the help of and was counseled by a liberal Protestant minister for nearly two years. He listened to her. She says she found some relief, but no significant changes occurred. She now comes to you at the suggestion of a Christian neighbor.

Problems:

1. After hearing her story, what sort of long-range counseling program do you begin to formulate in your mind?

2. What will you want to achieve during the first session? How?

3. List the problems that seem apparent already.

Homework

HE'S MARRIED BUT MASTURBATES

"I just can't seem to break the habit!" So said Josh during the first session when his wife had uttered the above statement and then had broken into tears. "She thinks," he continued, that there must be something wrong with her—that she can't satisfy me or something. I tell her that she is wrong, but you can see why she doesn't believe me. Before we were married, two years ago, masturbation had such a hold on me that I could hardly think straight. Now, however, I find myself doing it, but less frequently. Yet, as Flo says, I shouldn't masturbate at all. I don't want to, but how can I break the habit once for all?"

Problems:

1. Is Josh probably correct that he is grappling with a habit, or is that explanation too simplistic?

2. Assuming that he is correct, how would you help him to break the pattern?

3. Assuming that he is not, how would you discover the real cause?

4. Can Flo be enlisted to help? In what way(s)?

Homework

THE DISPIRITED MINISTER

"What's the use of going on? I work hard all of the time, but no one appreciates it! I visit constantly, but get criticized because I don't visit more. I sacrifice my family for the Lord's work, I preach my heart out, but who cares? I rarely see any change in the members of the congregation. My salary is so low that I can hardly survive, but when my wife took a part-time job the women in the church complained and she had to give it up. Everyone else in the congregation has two automobiles, many of them go to Florida for a couple of weeks each winter, and eat well. We are doing well when we eat hot dogs. I've had it! Tell me that I am right in thinking of leaving the ministry and getting a job outside. Couldn't I serve the Lord just as well (or perhaps better) there?

Problems:

1. How would you advise this man?

2. Is he contributing to his own problems? If so, how?

3. What might he do about the situation? Can you suggest any other options?

4. What are likely to be some of the central failures in his ministry?

5. Would you want to see his wife at future sessions? If so, for what purposes?

Homework

"SHE WON'T TALK"

"There isn't much to tell. She knows the answers, perhaps, but it looks like we'll never get them from her," said Mrs. Jones. "She has not spoken one word for five weeks," her husband added. Susan, their 16-year-old daughter, just sat there motionless, staring into space. "What should we do? School begins in two weeks. Something must happen soon. The physician examined her and is certain that there is no organic problem. He recommended a psychiatrist, but we hate to see Susan take that route. Is she in touch with reality? Pastor, what do you think? Can you tell us what to do next? I know this problem is probably more than you can handle, but which way should we go?"

Problems:

1. Will you take the case?

2. If so, on what assumption will you begin counseling?

3. How would you attempt to break the silence barrier?

4. How do you counsel when someone won't talk?

Homework

THE UNWILLING TEENAGER

"Question. What is your problem?
Answer. Nothing!
Question. What have you done about it?
Answer. Nothing!
Question. What do you want us to do about it?
Answer. Same thing!"

So read the last page of 16-year-old Phil's Personal Data Inventory. Before he entered the counseling room it was apparent that he would be difficult to deal with. You can lead a horse to water, but can you make him drink? God can. But how? What must the counselor do? From his parents' description of the problem (their Personal Data Inventory contained full answers) the difficulties revolved around rebellion, lack of communication, and underachievement leading to failure at school. They are all three sitting outside in the lobby; you have met none of them before.

Problems:

1. What do you tentatively plan to do when they enter the room?

2. Suppose you fail to get through to Phil. What will you advise his parents?

Homework

WHAT CAN YOU DO FOR A SINGLE GIRL WHO WANTS TO BE MARRIED?

"I never have dates. My father says that he expects me to die a spinster. I don't know what's wrong with me—. I'm not the most attractive girl, but I'm not the ugliest either. I want to be married and raise a family. Pastor, I can't advertise; what can I do?" So spoke Nancy, a 27-year-old Christian girl, who is very capable and works as a secretary in a law office. Nancy had tried many ways of "being where the boys are" (going to youth meetings, summer Bible conferences, etc.), all to no avail. It seems strange that Nancy should be in this plight. No one would have guessed it when she was the vivacious president of her youth group organizing the best meetings and parties that the youth of the church had known either before or afterwards. Yet, here she is, sitting forlorn in your office pleading for help. What can you tell her? The statistics don't seem to help!

Problems:

1. What will you need to discover first about Nancy?

2. What part could Nancy's father play in this situation?

3. Nancy's problem is not unique. Could she use her gifts to help both herself and others in some way?

4. What are some of the dangers that Nancy faces?

Homework

WHAT IS IT LIKE TO DIE?

Barbara, a thirteen-year-old member of your church comes to you soon after the death of her grandfather and asks, "What is it like to die?" She continues, "What it it like—that is, what does it feel like? Where does the spirit go; does it stay with the body until the resurrection? What does it mean that the 'silver cord is broken'?" Barbara has at least a dozen or so similar questions. At the conclusion she says, "I don't really understand what happened to Grandpa Green! Death saddens, but it also fascinates me. Then, at other times, I get terribly afraid when I think about death. Is there something wrong with me?"

Problems:

1. What sort of help does Barbara need?

2. Do you suspect that she has serious problems that she has not yet disclosed?

3. What will you attempt to do in this session?

Homework

"MY LIFE IS A BIG FAT ZERO!"

Midge is a 23-year-old, single working girl. She is a graduate of a Bible college and now works as a secretary at the same school.

On the Personal Data Inventory she describes herself as being "often—blue," "shy," and "lonely." She also adds: "I'm a nothing," and "I feel inferior." She says that she prays often but reads her Bible only occasionally.

As she sees it, this is the main problem: "My self concept is just absolutely zero. That may surprise you, but it is. My whole life has been a big, fat zero. Nobody notices me, nobody likes me, and nobody cares about me. I may as well be dead. I feel so inadequate. Even when I pray I can't find any relief. Probably the Lord doesn't even like me. But he is the one who made me this way, so maybe he does."

Problems:

1. Do you think Midge has identified her problem correctly?

2. Do you think she has leveled fully with you?

3. What can be done about her "self-concept"?

Homework

FUTURE FEAR

"I'm really confused about the future. To realize that I will be graduating soon and do not know what I will be doing next scares me a little." This is what seventeen-year-old Pete has said to you as the session opens. "My problem is that I don't know what I can do with my life. I don't really feel prepared for much," he explains.

Problems:

1. How many sessions are you likely to see Pete?

2. Do you think that he has any deep seated problems or patterns that need to be dealt with?

3. How would you proceed? What would be your first question?

Homework

DREAM WORLD

"I go into a dream world and fantasize about my high school days. Since I became a Christian six months ago I find myself worshiping Satan during these dreams," Christina tells you.

Christina is a young mother of twenty-five. "I enter it and leave it voluntarily, but lately I have been bothered by it. I play three or four roles that relate to my high school days. What has bothered me is that since I've become a Christian Cynthia (one of my roles) has started to worship Satan. When Cynthia talks to Carol and Carry (two more of my roles) she uses all sorts of dirty words and makes reference to lewd experiences she has had," Christina confides. "It's all very much like the books that I have been reading on the occult."

Problems:

1. What are some possible explanations for Christina's problem?

2. How can Christina stop "entering" the "dream world" once and for all?

3. Is closing the door on the "dream world" enough?

4. What would you tell her at this session?

Homework

FIRST DATE

"How do you ask a girl out? What do you talk about on a date? I'm interested in electronics, but girls aren't. Where can we go and what can we do?" fourteen-year-old David questions you vigorously.

Initial questions in response seem to indicate that there are no subtle undertones to his questions—he seems simply to want some answers to these questions. "But," you wonder, "how can I be sure?"

Problems:

1. How *can* you make sure?

2. How would you answer David's inquiries?

3. What do you think that these questions indicate?

Homework

UNERASED ITEM

"I have problems relating to people. They seem not to care about me. I tried everything to make friends but have failed," declares Luke. "I have doubts about my salvation, too. I don't seem to be able to do what the Bible tells me. Do you think that there is something wrong with me?" asks Luke for the second week in a row.

"Your homework is not complete again. But before we talk about that, why don't you tell me about this one note that you wrote down about not being able to see men in any stage of undress," you begin.

"Oh, that—well I was depressed when I wrote that. I was going to erase it. I get depressed because I can't do what God wants me to do and think about all sorts of things which cause it. It's nothing."

Problems:

1. Is Luke evading or is he telling the truth?

2. What is possibly behind this entry on the list?

3. Why didn't Luke erase the item?

4. What line of approach would you want to take?

Homework

THE TRAMP

"She is a tramp. I just know it. She won't tell me what she does on her dates or where she goes. She calls and tells me that she is at her girl friend's house for the night, and for all I know she is sleeping with some boy some place," declares Trudy's mother.

In response to that opening remark Trudy smiles acidly and says, "You tell him, Mother. You ought to know what my life is like. I *am* my mother's daughter."

"Would you believe those are the first words she has said to me for two months?! Look, Trudy, I love you. Why won't you love me? I ask nothing of you," sobs Mrs. Revere.

The Reveres have returned to your congregation after a five-year tour of service overseas with the Army. Lt. Col. Revere was one of your elders before being transferred.

Problems:

1. This is the sort of sticky situation into which the counselor must penetrate without driving deeper wedges. How?

2. Describe Mrs. Revere's attitudes.

3. How can the truth be learned?

4. What verse (in particular) suggests the solution to the basic problem that has brought about this difference?

Homework

SPECIAL REVELATION

"Now explain this to me again, Phil," the counselor inquires. "Why did you quit your job?"

"Because the Holy Spirit told me to," responds the 23-year-old fellow.

"And *how* did the Holy Spirit tell you?"

"He spoke to me. You know, I heard a voice. It always happens that way."

"Well, I don't understand. It's never happened to me, and there is no biblical reason to expect that it would happen to you. But let's quickly examine the results of this decision. Where do you live now?"

"Oh, I still live with my parents."

"And how much do you pay them for room and board?"

"I can't pay them anything now, because I don't have a job. I'm trusting the Lord."

"You mean you're trusting the Lord to get you a new source of income?"

"No, I'm trusting the Lord to provide for me and to take care of me. He told me to spend my time witnessing downtown, so that's what I do. I study the word and witness—You know, like the apostles in Acts 6. The Lord called me to it."

Problems:

1. How are you going to handle this one?

2. Is it better to deal with the doctrinal matters or to look for other possible causes for the difficulty?

3. What are some of the problems that are likely to be involved in this case?

4. What can be done to help Phil? Must anything else be done first?

Homework

TOO FAR GONE?

Haddie is a gray-haired lady who wanders the streets in a bewildered and disoriented world of her own. She is sixty-four years old, and upon further questioning you find out that she was once married and is the mother of two girls. She has come because she wants you to explain a tract that she found in the street that had your church address on it. You are now engaging her in a first counseling session to help her.

"My Mister was running around on me and I wouldn't give him a divorce. He had me committed to an institution and declared mentally incompetent because he convinced the doctor I did crazy things. . . . Maybe I did. I don't remember any more," she rambles.

That had been when she was thirty-five years old. She had been in and out of institutions for the next twenty years. Her husband had gotten a divorce and moved away to parts unknown with the two girls.

"I cried for six months and waited for such a long time to hear from any of them and then finally gave up hope," she sobs. "I still hurt so much inside that I don't know what to do."

Problems:

1. Where would you go from here?

2. What does Haddie need?

3. What do you think you can do for her?

Homework

SHOULD HE GO?

"My mother is so depressed and demanding that she has no friends left. It has been murder on us kids; I can't stand it any more." Tim, a seventeen-year-old boy, recently saved and attending your youth group, tells a story that goes back ten years. "My mother used to get like this when she didn't get her way with my dad." He goes on to tell of his father's increasing inability to cope with his own problems and the problems that she caused him. "He tried to get her to talk and all she would do is yell at him and tell him how stupid he was. After a while he came to believe it," Tim states.

"Then about two years ago, he went to the basement and hanged himself. Mom was yelling for him and finally went looking for him. She found him and after the funeral went to bed for a month," he continues.

Tim tells of alcoholism, raging anger, acute depression, and chronic depression. Her liberal minister avoids her and she won't take advice from anyone. Tim has had to wait on her constantly, and take care of his two younger brothers. He now declares that he is ready to move out of the house. He is asking your advice before taking the final step.

Problems:

1. What would you advise Tim?

2. Is there any hope in this case?

3. Tim says that he loves his mother in spite of everything and is concerned about his brothers, but that he "can't take any more." How can he best handle these concerns?

Homework

"I DON'T KNOW!"

"Well, John," says the counselor to the 16-year-old boy, "being expelled from school is a very serious matter. Why don't you tell me why you did this."

"There was only one reason," responds the slim, long-haired youth. "I got caught smoking grass on school property."

"I see. How long have you used marijuana?"

"It's been about six months, I guess."

"And why did you get into it originally, John? Why did you start using it?" the counselor inquires.

"Oh, I don't know. I guess it was because so many of my friends were into it. You know. I knew it was illegal and all, but it sounded like a good thing. So I got into it, that's all."

"Well, you knew it was illegal, you knew it displeased your parents, you knew it displeased God, but you still went ahead. Even on school grounds! Really, John, why did you continue in it for six months?"

"I don't know!"

Problems:

1. How would you evaluate this counselor?

2. What led to John's final response?

3. How might the counselor have elicited more usable data?

Homework

SHY?

Thirteen-year-old Ginny is aware that she is not well liked because (she says) she is "so quiet." "I want to have friends but it seems that they don't want me. I guess I'm just kind of shy and independent. For one thing, I don't like all those stupid activities that turn on the other kids. As far as I'm concerned, the church youth meetings and parties are immature!"

"What have you done to make friends, Ginny?" you inquire.

"Well, I try to make friends by going to meetings and so on, but I can't seem to get interested in what interests the others."

Problems:

1. What must Ginny be told?

2. Suppose that she is right about the youth group; how can she handle the problem differently?

3. Is Ginny shy? What does "shyness" often seem to indicate?

Homework

CAN'T KEEP JOBS

Matt is 41 years old. He is a professing Christian, the father of two girls. During the sixteen years of his marriage, he has had long stretches of unemployment, and three months ago, during the most recent period, when "financial problems and the arguments that ensued became too much for her to take," Fran (his wife) took his daughters and left him. They are now living with her mother. His wife makes no profession of faith.

His records show that Matt often received amounts of money from the church he attends. But a month ago he got a 30-hour-per-week job, and has kept it since.

Matt describes his problem this way: "I want to get back with my family and be the husband I never was. This time I mean business, but my wife doesn't want to talk with me. She considers me a bum. How can I change and get out of this mess?"

Problems:

1. Starting with Matt's question, what would you say in response?

2. What would be your basic counsel to him?

3. How would you seek to involve Fran?

Homework

"WE HAVE A PERFECT MARRIAGE!"

Janet and Perry are Christians in their early forties. On his Personal Data Inventory Perry writes: "We have no major problems. I came only because of my wife's incessant requests. I don't know what she gets so uptight about. I like everything just as it is. I think we have a great marriage. Help her to see this and we'll all be O.K."

Janet sees the situation quite differently. She reports strong feelings of depression, bitterness, and a sense of being "smothered." She says Perry is "non-communicative," and concludes, "one thing that really irritates me is his close attachment to his parents. We see them at least twice a week, and have been going on vacation with them every year for 14 years. Sometimes I wonder if I married Perry or his parents!"

Problems:

1. How can Perry be shown (or brought to admit) that there are problems to solve?

2. Is Janet exaggerating, perhaps just to get a few things straightened out?

3. Where do you begin, and with whom?

Homework

"WE CAN'T LIVE TOGETHER"

Mike and Lydia are in their late 30's, the parents of two small sons. About a year ago they were separated for two months. (She says because of his drunkenness and irresponsibility.)

At that time she had to work and got to know a Christian woman. She was presented the claims of Christ, and subsequently professed faith in Him. The same Christian woman arranged for Mike to speak with an elder from the church. Mike agreed, and after a few sessions also professed faith in Christ.

Everything appeared to change. They became reconciled with each other, and went back to live together. But in a month's time the roof blew off the house! Mike allegedly has reverted to his old behavior—drinking, missing work, etc.—and within a short time stopped coming to church.

Neither one expects much from your counseling. They were persuaded by a Christian friend to come, and make a last-ditch effort.

She says, "I don't see how I can live with an irresponsible drunk!"

He says, "She constantly criticizes me. She makes a federal case out of everything; I was drunk only *once*. The wonder is that I haven't gotten drunk more often!"

Problems:

1. What do Mike and Lydia need to receive in this first session?

2. The homework assignment will be critical. What elements *must* it include?

—

3. Does Mike's reversion indicate that his profession of faith was false?

Homework

FEAR OF SEX

Tom and Jean (21 and 20) are Christians who have been married for eighteen months. They were referred to you by another pastor who couldn't handle the problem.

The problem? Tom summed it up this way: "Jean is always shaking and getting hysterical whenever I want to have sex. She says, 'I can't overcome the fears I have of sex.' " Jean confirms the truth of his statement and adds, "I just don't know what comes over me." Tom is obviously very frustrated. He says that he tries to be patient, but the patience frequently gives way to his quick temper. He has remained faithful to Jean, but confesses on the Personal Data Inventory that he is often troubled by lustful thoughts toward other women.

In answer to the question, "Is there any physical aspect to the problem?" Tom replies, "When a gynecologist attempted to examine Jean, he *could not* because she was 'afraid.' "

They both say that they want to solve this problem and will cooperate in anything that you tell them to do, but they simply don't know what to do next.

Problems:

1. What do you think is Jean's problem (in general)?

2. What would you tell them in this first session?

3. What additional data would you seek?

4. How would you try to establish hope?

5. What plan would you lay out?

6. How would you relate to the other pastor?

Homework

ABORTION?

Debbie, a sixteen-year-old high school student, who makes a sound profession of faith, and her mother, who is also a member of your church, have come, as Mom puts it, for "advice about a theological matter." The basic facts are: Debbie was raped several weeks ago by a fellow high school student with a different racial background. She is pregnant. Debbie asks, "Would I be sinning if I have an abortion?" She says she thinks the circumstances surrounding her case would justify an abortion, but she isn't sure. In preliminary questioning you notice that Debbie seems quite confused about the way that she reached this tentative conclusion, and that her mother seems to have a much better grasp of the pro-abortion arguments.

Problems:

1. What would you do? Give advice? If so, what?

2. Would you offer to do more?

3. Do you think that Debbie is the only one who might need counseling?

4. Where is dad? Do you think that it is strange that he is not present at a time like this?

Homework

A DRUNKEN MOTHER

Vivian, a seventeen-year-old girl who attends the church youth meetings and has become a Christian, comes seeking help for herself and her younger brother and sister. She explains that her mother is a drunkard and unfit to raise them. The problem, she says, centers upon her mother's alcoholic rages that have become the everyday occurrence in their home. Divorced eight years ago, the mother moved into town, having obtained custody of the three children, but she has no real means of support. She began to drink, and then married a drunk that she met in one of the bars that she frequented. Vivian says that ever since things have become worse and worse. About six months ago her step-father left for parts unknown and her mother developed a terrible temper after that.

What brought Vivian at this time was the worst of the temper displays. The mother threw a portable TV at the youngest child, barely missing him, and beating him literally until he bled.

Problems:

1. What would you tell Vivian?

2. What steps would you take next?

Homework

IMAGINATION?

Janice, bursting into tears before she makes her opening remarks, charges that her husband has "improper relationships" with several (four) women in their church. Cedrick (her husband) says that there are no real problems except with his wife's attitude. As the session develops, it becomes clear that the wife has confronted each of these women in the congregation with her charges. These women variously became angered, tried to explain that they were only friendly (they worked on the same committee), etc., but all four strongly denied any impropriety on their part or by Cedrick. Cedrick insists that there is no significant problem except his wife's imagination and jealousy. Counseling further disclosed that they had gone for six months to a Christian psychologist. There were no positive results. They both claim that he stated that their case was hopeless. Cedrick and Janice agreed that they had reached the conclusion that they were as they were because that was the way God had made them. "And, after all," Cedrick said, "married life is just one set of problems after another."

Problems:

1. What emphasis and tone would you like to see in this first session?

2. Would it be more important to stress data gathering now or later on? If later, when? How?

3. If you opt for data gathering later on, what goals would you have for this session?

Homework

WHAT DO I DO NOW?

"What is my responsibility to my husband now that he has filed for a divorce?" Mrs. Williams, the 38-year-old member of a neighboring conservative congregation comes to you, seeking advice. She asks, "What should I do? My husband, Reggie, has filed for divorce. I am a Christian and my husband has made a profession of faith also. But he left me and obtained a legal separation six months ago. Before the separation we counseled with our pastor for about five months. He only listened to us; never told us what to do or how to get out of the mess. Reggie finally quit and left. Reggie says that he does not love me any more. Can you help me?" In addition, Mrs. Williams tells you that she has legal rights to the children and that her husband has stopped coming to church. When he comes to see the children he wants to have sexual relations with her. She wonders whether she should agree to this request.

Problems:

1. What further information would you seek?

2. Assume you obtain certain additional data; built on that and what you learn from the case presentation, what advice would you give Mrs. Williams?

3. What is your responsibility to Mrs. Williams' pastor? How would you handle that responsibility in this session? Later on?

Homework

CAN TWO FAMILIES BECOME ONE?

Ray and Alice, Christians and members of your congregation, are bewildered and confused. They seem to be at the end of their rope. They do not know how to bring peace to their home. The antagonism of their children toward one another truly seems grave. The children are from two families who have come together following the deaths of spouses and the consequent remarriage of their parents. The children (six in all; ages six to eighteen) are showing open rebellion to parental authority and hatred for one another. The house is divided. The parents, married for two years, express disbelief that this is happening in their home, because they *never* had problems in their previous marriages. Can anything be done? A house divided against itself cannot stand.

Problems:

1. Would you want to see the children? Soon? Or would you elect to work with the parents first?

2. What sort of program would you think might be needed to begin solving this problem?

Homework

"TOO WEAK"

Bill and Jean, a middle-aged couple, members of an independent congregation some distance from yours, waste no time getting to the point. They are on the verge of separation after nineteen years of marriage. Jean complains, "Pastor, we have not had sexual relations for the last five months. Three years ago, not long after we were saved, I discovered that Bill had been reading pornography. At first this consisted of 'nature' magazines; now he is importing hard core stuff from Denmark! He claims that I am sexually uninteresting and that he no longer desires me!"

Bill acknowledges that what she says is true, but adds, "That is not the whole story. We have had trouble for a long time, ever since Jean was unfaithful to me in the second year of our marriage."

Jean wants to save the marriage, but she is frustrated. She says that Bill is not interested in giving up his pornography. She does admit that he has made attempts. "Twice he made fresh starts after dedications in revival meetings. He tore up the stuff and threw it away. That was my idea in getting him to go to the meetings. But, he is too weak to stick to his new commitments." She also complains, "I have found it necessary to become the spiritual leader in our home. *I* have to urge the children to go to church, *I* have to hold family devotions, etc."

Bill claims that he wants a divorce. "I have a good job; I'll support her and the children. All that I ask is for you to get her off my back!"

Problems:

1. What would be your goals for this session?

2. Do you see any hope for this marriage? If so, state in what (be specific).

3. With whom would you probably speak most in this session?

4. Would it be good to concentrate on data gathering at this session?

Homework

RINGWORM

"Pastor, we've got an embarrassing problem. You see . . . uh . . . we . . . I . . . ."

"He's got ringworm on his penis and we haven't had intercourse for over three weeks. The doctor says it's a stubborn case, and warned us that it might be some time yet before we could expect to have relations again. But we both want to have relations badly."

"She thinks that . . . uh . . . mutual masturbation—bringing each other to orgasm—would solve the problem. I'm not sure that that is Christian. What do you think, Pastor?"

Problems:

1. Does the Bible speak to this problem? Directly? By implication?

2. What advice would you give?

3. How many sessions would you have?

4. Could there be more to this situation than meets the eye? How would you find out?

Homework

"I'M GOING TO HELL"

"I'm afraid that I'm going to hell," were Gary's opening words. Gary recently began attending your church. He continues, "Last night I got drunk and when I came home my mother was really uptight. She thinks that I should be put into a mental hospital." Gary's appearance eloquently supplemented the story of his 28 years of frustrations and discouragement. Grossly overweight, dishevelled and dirty, he was the very picture of a hopeless case. Still living with his parents, he had never held a steady job and had no prospects for one. He declared he was subject to occasional flashbacks because of his experimentation with drugs a few years back. He claimed to be the only Christian in his home, but his testimony to his parents, needless to say, was nil. Numerous attempts to reform—which always fizzled—left his parents skeptical over his talk of "sorrow" or "repentance" and "change." This skepticism had burrowed its way into his own heart: "I can't go on this way. I want to repent, but I don't feel that God will forgive me any more. I have repented so often in the past."

Problems:

1. What does "repentance" seem to mean to Gary?

2. How would you handle Gary's fear of going to hell?

3. Where would you begin with him?

Homework

"I CAN'T TAKE IT"

"Reverend, I'm so ashamed of it. It has been destroying our marriage from the beginning." Premarital sex with her husband-to-be, to whom she had now been married for twelve years, was Cecelia's simple explanation for her wrecked marriage. From further questioning, you discover that there has never been much communication between Cecelia and her husband, Hugh, and none when the subject of their marriage was involved. Hugh, she says, is exceedingly proud, and refuses to admit that there is anything wrong with their marriage. She even fears that Hugh will discover that she has discussed their problems with a third party—yet she wants you to help her. She is desperate: "I just can't go on this way any longer. Our children are old enough to realize something terrible is wrong, and *I* can't take it any longer emotionally."

Problems:

1. What do you think the counselor should do?

2. Could Cecelia's view be correct?

3. What of Hugh?

4. What is the danger in this case?

Homework

SLIM EVIDENCE

Lawrence and Pat have been married seventeen years. Five years ago they joined your church. Ten years ago Lawrence cheated on Pat, having sexual relations with her sister. This went on for a year and a half before it surfaced. He gave up the sister and asked Pat to return to him, and she did. About two and a half months ago Pat had a phone call. The man identified himself as "Joe from the plant." He told her that Lawrence was running around with another woman over his lunch hour (he works three to eleven). She began accusing him and things have rapidly deteriorated. He says, "It is just not true." A few other coincidental factors have confirmed Pat's suspicions. Lawrence says, "there is nothing to confirm." They are visibly hostile, especially Pat. Their conversation sounds like this:

Pat: "This time you know that I have the truth."

Lawrence: "No, it's not. I'm not running around."

Pat: "You are and I know it. You don't live with someone seventeen years and not know when something is wrong. You beat me. You did it before. You can't stand to touch me."

Lawrence: "Yes, I hit you. Every time I walk in the house you badger me. What do you expect me to do? Who wants to touch a vixen?"

Pat: "Pastor, you ask my daughter how he is—how he always has been."

Problems:

1. Where is the pastor?

2. What would you tell Pat about anonymous phone calls?

3. How can the issue be resolved?

4. Will you be able to work on the issue before dealing with the re-lationship?

Homework

SHOW ME HOW

Bruce and Maggie appear with their daughter, Karen. The pastor is surprised; he expected only the parents.

Counselor: "Why are you here, Karen?" (Shrug of shoulders)

Maggie: "I asked her to come. She and I can't get along and it is wrecking our home."

Counselor: "Do you see a problem between you and Mom?"

Karen: "Um, yes."

Counselor: "Would you say there is animosity between you and Mom?"

Karen: (Hesitating, then) "Much!"

Counselor: "Why is there this problem with Mom?"

Karen: "I don't know."

"Counselor: "Do you have this problem with anyone else?"

Karen: "No."

Counselor: "Karen, you know you are to honor your mother. It is sin not to. Do you see this as sin?"

Karen: "Yes."

Counselor: "Why haven't you made a move to right this situation?"

Karen: "I don't know how."

Problems:

1. Is this counseling session going anywhere? Where?

2. Where is the counselor going wrong?

3. How would you have opened the session?

Homework

A BLACK EYE

Dave and Sue are a young couple who visited your church last Sunday. Thursday evening you call on them and during the initial pleasantries you sense that your offhand remark about Sue's black eye did not sit well. You secretly regret making it. But as you begin to mention the Bible as a prelude to talking to them about their relationship to Christ, the dam suddenly breaks: "The Bible!" Sue shouts. "That's what he needs. But I doubt that even the Bible would help a man like him!"

In the discussion that ensues you learn that two days ago Dave had beaten Sue severely and that she had called the police. As a result he had appeared before a judge this very morning. Sue says that she is planning to divorce Dave as soon as she can save enough money to leave him, and she plans to take only their five-year-old girl, Ann (they have two children besides: Dave, Jr., 4, and Adam, 6). Dave bitterly blames Sue for all of their problems: "She has had three affairs in the six years of our marriage!" Sue responds (darkly) stating that Dave has "killed any love she ever had by his gross inconsiderateness and his weak leadership in the home."

Problems:

1. What should you try to accomplish on this visit?

2. Do you think that divorce is inevitable?

3. What is the possible significance of Sue's plans?

4. What would be a tentative agenda if (1) both agreed to counseling? (2) Sue only agreed? (3) Dave only agreed?

Homework

EMPATHY

"My situation is so different," Laurie explained. Laurie, the wife of a young seminarian, had come (she said) because "I feel obligated to David to keep working, since I want him to be able to concentrate on school. I would never forgive myself if I quit my job, because he would have to reduce his class load in order to work, and I know that he wouldn't get as much out of school. But Pastor, I tell you, my job is impossible! I can't advance because I'm pegged as being temporary. I can't tell David or he'll tell me to quit. Less qualified men are promoted before me because, as my boss seemed happy to explain, 'a man's voice on the phone commands more respect, and therefore, is more valuable to the company.' And to top it off, I get no encouragement in the work that I am doing. I am losing my self-confidence; what shall I do?"

Laurie's story tugs at your heart; not long ago you and your wife were in nearly an identical situation. You can empathize with her and are inclined to advise her that she might change jobs at the earliest opportunity. But you are not sure; "Is there more that can be done for Laurie?" you wonder.

Problems:

1. Is your inclination sound?

2. What dangers of overidentification are there in counseling? What advantages in identification?

3. How can Laurie best be helped?

4. Was it wise to counsel her alone, or should her husband have been present?

5. What differences might her husband's presence have made?

Homework

"PLEASE LISTEN"

"I know that you can't help me, but just *please* listen," begged Lena in a tone of despair. "I don't know what to do. I have to talk to someone. I am sick of it all." Lena then proceeds to describe a life of immorality, deception, and failure that, she says, "makes Watergate look like an old ladies' tea party." When Lena was 14, she and some of her friends thought that it would be fun to seduce a married man. They made a pact to do so. Each was to come back and report. Lena dressed up and sneaked out to a local bar. She was successful, and to her amazement the man gave her ten dollars. She returned to report this to her friends, to discover that it was all a hoax on their part. Upon finding out that she had gone through with it, they dropped her like a hot potato in fear. Lena then decided to show them and made herself available to each of their fathers. Again to her amazement, they agreed and paid her to keep quiet. In time, her "exploits" became a way of life which led to prostitution, two illegitimate children, three abortions, and now her doctor has told her that she has cancer. "There is just no hope for me at all. My life is too messed up and I am too far gone to do anything about it all!"

Problems:

1. Beyond her need for the gospel, what is Lena's greatest need?

2. How would you seek to evangelize her?

3. Assuming that she became a Christian, how would you want to help her afterwards?

4. What place could your local congregation play in helping Lena?

Homework

"WHERE DO WE GO FROM HERE?"

Both Jerry and Carla are professed Christians, have been married for six years, have one two-year-old daughter named Kelly, and currently are living with Carla's widowed mother. Last Wednesday morning the women left Kelly with Jerry while they went shopping, and upon returning home found Kelly badly bruised. On the way to the hospital, Jerry explained that Kelly had fallen down the stairs. Carla challenged his story when the X-rays showed that Kelly had a fractured arm, and after much argumentation Jerry confessed that he had lost his temper when Kelly had refused to stop crying and had thrown her against the wall. In telling the story, Carla showed deep bitterness against Jerry. Jerry's attitude seems cool and guarded. He does not seem sorry or repentant. Carla asks, "Where do we go from here?"

Problems:

1. Carla's question was a good one. Would you answer it directly? Now? Later? How?

2. What do you suspect are some of the dimensions of Jerry's problems?

3. How would you begin to gather data additional to those given by Carla?

Homework

ALL THINGS NEW?

A very well-educated, attractive couple comes to you because they know that you do Christian counseling. Their source of information was a member of your congregation who teaches with the husband in a local university. They are members of a well-established local church which is known for its liberal views. However, they explain that it is out of habit and sentimentality for the church that they attend. They tell you that they both have recently become Christians and that is when the trouble started.

They realized that since they are now new creations in Christ Jesus, that they have already changed significantly and that they will change even more. They declare that they are now no longer compatible. Sexual relations no longer occur. They say that they believe that through the new insights that they have gained since becoming Christians they have discovered that they married for all the wrong reasons, and that they now realize that they made a bad decision in choosing one another as partners. They are hopeful that you can advise them on the proper kind of divorce settlement, because they want to do the right thing by one another, and because if they do, they feel that God will surely lead them to "more suitable Christian mates."

Problems:

1. What, above all else, do you want to know first?

2. What will you attempt to do for them?

3. How large a part of their problem would you suspect that their church affiliation might be?

Homework

"I'VE COMMITTED
THE UNPARDONABLE SIN"

Before you can even say "hello" Rachel bursts into tears, saying, "Oh! Pastor, help me! I've committed the unforgivable sin. I know that there is no forgiveness, but how can I live with the fact?" With a note of desperation and fear, Rachel, a young girl who recently started attending services at your church, tells you her story.

"I know that when I was thirteen I became a Christian, but then, in high school, I started to use drugs. It all started with diet pills and got worse. When I was seventeen I ran away from home and hitched around the country for a couple of years. I slept with anyone that I could and finally gave birth to an illegitimate child. While in the hospital a preacher came to see me, and I again accepted Christ. I went home and all was forgiven. I married about a year later and we had two children, very close together. There were financial difficulties, and out of nowhere the father of my illegitimate child showed up. That was a year ago.

Since then we have been all over the place together. One night, about six weeks ago I found a Bible in the house where we were, and my conscience started bothering me. I read it and my adultery again came to my mind. Tom dumped me a week later because I wouldn't sleep with him, and I realized that my unfaithfulness to God and to my husband were not forgivable. Knowing that I have committed the unpardonable sin has almost driven me crazy this past month. Can you help me to deal with it?"

Problems:

1. Doctrinally, Rachel is far off the mark in several ways. Is dealing with this doctrinal defectiveness the best approach to her problems?

2. What are Rachel's problems?

3. How will you help her to face them?

Homework

"GOD IS PICKING ON ME"

It was a major accomplishment to get 25-year-old Andy into your study for counseling. He had already broken two appointments and had finally come only because your secretary had called him on the phone, awakening him twenty minutes before his 11 a.m. appointment.

Once he was sitting in the study, however, he was eager to spell out his story of loneliness, self-pity, and frustration. As he put it, "Everything stems from one problem." By way of simplification he explains: "Pastor, I'm overweight; I haven't been able to get a date for years. I don't have anything to look forward to and I'm ashamed of my past—especially my relation to my parents. I have trouble keeping a job, and I feel like God is picking on me. If He had not made me fat, none of these problems would have arisen!"

You sense a large amount of self-pity and self-righteousness in Andy's words. Some initial probing confirms your suspicions. Andy has come to blame his every failure on his obesity. And even in this matter he seems unwilling to assume any responsibility. He continues: "I've tried dozens of times to lose weight, but I just can't. My doctor says that I have no glandular or hormonal problem, but I'm sure there must be a deep underlying reason why I can't lose weight. Whenever I think that I'm beginning to get somewhere with a girl, my weight problem seems to mess it up."

Problems:

1. What does Andy need to know?

2. What do you think is at the bottom of his weight problem?

3. Would loneliness, self-pity, etc., be more likely to be chicken or egg?

4. How can the counselor fry the egg and bring the process to a halt?

Homework

"OUR LAST HOPE"

"I've filed for divorce, but I don't think that is the right thing to do. You are our last hope; help us, Pastor," pleads Joan.

Joan and Bill have come expecting little help. They had been raised in the same evangelical church, where they made a profession of faith. But when they married five years ago, they moved and never became a part of a Bible teaching congregation. They drifted, and ultimately reached this point. Now, the church is their last resort (they looked you up in the yellow pages).

Bill says, "Our problems began when I was laid off at work. I couldn't find another job. So I began to feel guilty, and to drown my feelings I started to drink and to stay away; I couldn't face Joan and the family that I couldn't support. Joan was bringing in all of the money. I got unemployment compensation, but I drank it all up. One day, feeling especially sorry for myself, I met a girl in a bar, and . . . well, anyway, . . . the next thing I knew a cop hit me with a statutory rape charge," he blurted out, and began to cry.

"I left him. I figured that if he had to turn to a seventeen-year-old high school dropout, he didn't need me! Then I realized how much I loved him, so a week later I moved back," Joan explained.

"The charges were dropped and I was released. But still no job; then Joan became pregnant. . . ."

Joan, now also weeping, tells of an abortion: "I couldn't lose my job; how could we live?"

"It seems that I have brought nothing but sorrow to Joan. I should let her get the divorce; I don't deserve her," Bill concludes.

"Is there no hope?" asks Joan.

Problems:

1. What is the greatest need at this point?

2. How would you meet that need?

3. What would you do next, assuming that this need could be met successfully?

4. Would you work mainly with Joan or with Bill at this session?

Homework

"GET ME OUT OF THIS MESS"

Jane, 22 years old, attends your church twice. On her second visit at services you begin to ask where she is from, what she is doing, etc. She immediately requests an appointment to "talk about the mess that I am in."

At her first session she says that she recently became a Christian and is concerned about her life. Before this she was divorced from a teenage marriage which produced two children. She has custody of the children and the father doesn't care about them at all. She is now pregnant as the result of an affair with Mark, a friend of her brother. Mark is two years younger than she. She doesn't believe that he is a Christian, yet he talks about God. She has a good relation with his parents, but her relation with the boy has worn thin. She sobs, "What shall I do?" She's afraid of marriage, yet she wants to marry. She says, "I think that I love Mark, but I am not so sure that I respect him. Reverend, can you get me out of this mess?"

Problems:

1. What would you do next?

2. What part could your congregation play in helping out in this situation?

3. How would you advise her to proceed in the relationship with Mark?

4. What would your goals for Joan be?

Homework

"PLEASE HELP"

"Pastor, I've never told anyone, but I've got to tell you now. I can't keep it to myself any longer. I'm . . . I'm . . . I'm a queer!" Barry got up, walked to the window, and, looking out, continued, "Since my early teens I've been involved. My father and my older brother both were involved first and then they involved me. I got away from them when I went to college, but last year I got into it again with another student. Now I'm so deeply into it I don't know what I'll do. And when I graduate this spring I'm headed for seminary. I want to stop. But every time I try, I find that I can't. Please help me, Pastor. Is here any hope for a homosexual?" Incidentally, Barry and his entire family are members of your congregation. His brother plays the organ, and his father is an elder.

Problems:

1. What do you do next?

2. How will you proceed with Barry's family?

3. Assuming Barry is sincere, how will you help him?

Homework

"MY HUSBAND'S A PEEPING TOM"

"He is, he's a peeping Tom!" Shirley shouted through her tears.

"It's not true," Les responded. "She once saw me noticing a woman disrobing at an open window two years ago—How could I help it? There she was, I didn't look for her! It was simply a coincidence."

"But he goes out at nights—why do you think he goes out at nights if he's not? He won't tell me why."

"Pastor, I told her until I got blue in the face why I went out, and she never believed me; so I just don't tell her anything any more. What's the use?"

"Well, tell him about last Tuesday then!"

"I've told you a dozen times; it wasn't the way you took it."

"Oh, wasn't it? Then why did you buy those binoculars? Pastor, last Tuesday I found a pair of brand new binoculars in the car, the car he uses almost every night!"

Problems:

1. Where do you go from here?

2. Is Les a peeping Tom? How will you discover the truth?

3. What must you tell Shirley?

Homework

"MY BAGS ARE PACKED"

"All right, you'd better have something worth saying, Pastor, because if you don't I'm leaving him—my bags are packed and in the trunk of my car! Look at him grovelling, snivelling, pleading —who would even want to go on living with a man like that?"

"Please, Pastor, help us. I don't want Wilma to leave. I love her. It's true that I haven't been much of a husband or much of a man or a leader, but I love her. I'll do anything, *anything*, Wilma, please don't leave," begged Stanley as he clutched Wilma's arm.

Wilma, in disgust, pulled her arm free, folded her arms across her chest, and sneered, "Well, Pastor, you told me to come here before leaving him when he called you. What have you got to say? It had better be good, or else!"

Problems:

1. O.K., now it's your turn. In the space below, outline your speech (obviously, Rogerianism won't work with Wilma!).

Homework

"HIS TEACHER SAYS THAT WE DO NOT SPEND ENOUGH TIME WITH HIM . . ."

"She says that he is acting up in order to get attention," Freda continued. "Do you think she could be right? We *try* to take time to talk to Tommy every day and his father plays with him. How much *more* time do you think that we should spend? Or, is the teacher missing the boat altogether? After all, this is only her first year of teaching; she may be guessing."

Tommy's mother was concerned about the reports of her son's bad discipline at Christian school. Tommy was accused of repeatedly disrupting the third grade class. Yet, at home she reported that he gave his parents no more than the normal disciplinary problems. Where does the difficulty lie?

Problems:

1. How would you discover whether Tommy's disciplinary problems were usual or greater than usual?

2. What would you do to meet these?

3. Is it important that Tommy and his father did not come?

Homework

CAN'T CONTROL HIS WIFE

You could sympathize fully with Mr. Wilson when his 45-year-old wife majestically swept into the study a step in front of her husband, and tried —not entirely without success—to arrogate you to the counselee's chair.

"Good morning," she boomed. "We can't imagine why you wanted to talk with us!" Mr. Wilson shook his head helplessly in disgust over her shoulder as you returned her greeting.

The Wilsons, who had been members of a sound church across the state, had just moved into your town and had joined your church three months ago. In the meanwhile you had received a letter from their previous pastor indicating that he had been counseling them about their marriage and suggesting that you might pick up where he had been forced to leave off. His recommendation had led you to invite them to your study today.

Before ten minutes had passed (in which you explained your purpose and offered to continue the counseling) you had become painfully aware of at least one major problem: Mr. Wilson's total failure to control his wife. She constantly took the initiative, occasionally answered questions addressed to him and, in general, showed that she, rather than he, was in charge of the marriage.

The Wilsons did accept your offer and told the story of a steadily deteriorating marriage that had reached the point where Mr. Wilson was looking for excuses to stay away from home: "Of what use am I anyway?" he asked. "She runs the house, the children don't recognize my authority, and my only value is that of a breadwinner!"

118

Problems:

1. Who (if either) will be your principal target for discussion, questions, etc., in this first session?

2. Sketch out an *ideal* program for the next four or five counseling sessions.

3. How will you gain and maintain control of the counseling sessions?

Homework

"I'M PRETTY SMART"

"Hi! I'm God; what's your name?" was 10-year-old Jimmy's opening line. "You preachers sure are in a cushy job. I thought of trying it once, but I concluded that the work was not equal to my ability. I'm pretty smart, you know. My old man says I'm precocious."

Jimmy is here because of severe behavior problems. He is out of control, both at home and at school. His last escapade consisted of stealing a car, sideswiping a half dozen others, and ending up on top of a fire hydrant. As a mother and two children fled his path, one of the children was injured, but not severely, from a fall.

His parents cringe at his words, mother turning crimson and dad shrugging his shoulders helplessly. Both are professors at a local university and have been referred to you by a member of your congregation who teaches in the same department as Mr. Stevens, Jimmy's father. "We have given up all hope for him," he says. "We were intending to put him away when Charlie told us about you. We are desperate; that's why we're here." Mrs. Stevens added: "We don't believe the way you do, but we have faith."

"Go ahead, Preach, help them. They're the ones who need help. I'm O.K.—just hyperactive. That's what the shrink said. Go ahead, Daddy dear, tell the man all about me, and if you miss anything I'll fill it in for you. By the way, Rev, do you have a cigar?"

Problems:

1. Will you begin by taking on Jimmy or by handling his parents?

2. From what you know of him, how would you describe Jimmy's problem?

3. Are these parents likely to be cooperative?

4. How can you evangelize them?

Homework

PART TWO

SESSIONS IN PROCESS

FROM BAD TO WORSE

"I'm sorry that the situation with your boss didn't improve, Leon," the counselor says sadly. Did you ask for forgiveness like we suggested?"

"Yes, just like you recommended," responds the dejected 43-year-old carpenter. "And he only used it as an occasion to yell at me more. He's been on my back all week. I may lose my job over it."

"Well, I guess that you will just have to be patient. But how about things with your wife? That's even a more central concern for us."

"I know. But the news there is even worse. She won't agree to *anything* I suggest. She refuses to have family conferences, she refuses to go to church with me, and she still refuses to come in here. It seems like things are getting worse each day. I don't know why the Lord is doing it."

"Hasn't your communication with each other improved at all?"

"No, it's been getting worse!"

"Hmm. That's a bad sign. I guess you just have to keep trying the same things. It might just take a long time to work out. I want you to know that I'll be praying for you."

Problems:

1. What is a major factor in Leon's continued discouragement?

2. What is the striking problem in this counseling case?

3. What must be done about it? Is it too late?

Homework

"I'VE BEEN THINKING ABOUT YOU"

Joan, the attractive 31-year-old mother of two children, has been attending your church for about three months. She is not a member. After some initial counseling, she claims to have come to faith in Christ. She seems to have made some progress in beginning to live as a Christian and recently expressed interest in making a public profession of faith.

All efforts to meet her husband have failed. He says that, "he doesn't want to talk with any preacher."

Joan now seeks further counseling, this time concerning her marriage; she says that she has uncovered evidence that her husband is unfaithful to her. The two, she claims, have been drifting further apart every day. You advised her to confront him with the charge.

During conversation at church on the Sunday following the counseling session at which she offered this revelation, Joan made the following two surprisingly affectionate comments, "Pastor, I just *love* to spend time with you!" and "I think about you often." (Incidentally, you have another counseling session with Joan scheduled for two days hence.)

Problems:

1. What would you say in reply (if anything)?

2. What would your next step(s) be?

3. How would your counseling goals, methods, and relationship change?

_____

Homework

"I . . . WALKED OUT"

"Now let me get this right," says the counselor. "You only had three conference tables, and two of them blew up in arguments?"

"Yes, that's right," Paul and Jan reply simultaneously. "And what's more, the third one wasn't very profitable," Paul adds.

"What caused the first blowup?"

"Well, we were talking about finances, and I got mad at something Jan said."

"What was that, Jan?"

"I just said that we are in financial trouble now because Paul has never helped me or given me *any* leadership in organizing the budget."

"And when I saw her attitude I didn't want to talk any more," Paul blurts out. "Besides, it wouldn't have been any use. She didn't want to talk. She wanted to criticize."

"Now was the second blowup over the same issue?" asks the counselor.

"No, it was different," says Jan. "I wanted to discuss Paul's defensiveness with him. The thing that happened at the first conference is typical for him. Whenever Paul's failures are mentioned, he becomes defensive and stops talking."

"And what happened when she mentioned this, Paul?"

"I got mad and walked out. I don't have to stand for that kind of stuff!"

128

Problems:

1. Who was at fault in the failure of the family conferences? How?

2. Do you think that this counselor used family conferences effectively?

3. How can he help them to avoid such failures in the future?

4. In what way could the counselor capitalize upon these failures to help his counselees?

Homework

"DADDY DOESN'T MAKE ME"

"Have the suggestions for disciplining little Tina been helping?" the counselor inquires of Liz, a 27-year-old mother.

"Well, I think they've been of some help, but I always run into problems. When I'm home alone with Tina, things go better, but then my husband comes home and everything falls apart."

"Have you talked with him about these new principles of discipline?"

"I've tried to, but he doesn't like the ideas. I just think that he doesn't really understand. He says that little girls shouldn't have to receive punishment like that. And Tina *knows* what he thinks. So she gets away with murder when he's home. It just totally undoes everything that I do in the day. And then she says to me, 'Daddy doesn't make me do this.' "

"Well, you say that you've talked with your husband a little, but how hard have you tried?"

"Not very much, I guess. But I know that if I push him we'll only end up in a fight. Besides, I don't know how to get it across to him the way you explained it to me."

130

Problems:

1. This problem is missing an obvious factor; can you identify it?

2. How would you handle the problem at this point? How would you have started out?

3. If Liz's husband really "doesn't like" your "ideas" of discipline, what can be done?

Homework

"IT'S BEEN TWO DAYS"

"Now Linda, let's check out your homework," the counselor says to the 35-year-old woman. "Did you make a schedule for the week?"

"Yes, here it is," responds the attractive woman who had come because of depression problems.

"I see, now is this the projected schedule for you to follow every week?"

"Oh no. It's just a record of what I did this week. Wasn't that the assignment?"

"No, Linda, I wanted you to plan ahead and put profitable activities into your week. I thought I made that clear."

"Oh, I'm sorry," said Linda, fluttering her eyelashes.

"That's all right. Just do it for next week. Now, what about the pamphlet on worry? Did you read that?"

"Well, I read most of it."

"And did it help you?"

"Yes."

"How?"

"I can't remember right now," she responds. "It's been two days since I looked at it."

Problems:

1. What is happening here?

2. How has the counselor been affected?

3. Is he helping Linda?

4. What do you think is behind Linda's depression?

5. What does the counselor need to do?

Homework

"ALL I COULD THINK OF"

"I asked you to make a list of specific sins, Carl," says the counselor. "Do you have it ready?"

"Yes. It's not a long list, but here it is," responds the 48-year-old husband and father.

"Good. Let's see what some of them are. Hmm, you list concern about your daughter's school work as a sin? That's not exactly the type of thing we were after, but let's look at the rest. You say 'I think about parents too much (they are old and poor).' Then you say 'I work too hard.' Tell me Carl, is this what you think of when I mention sins?"

"Well, those things really aren't that bad I guess," he calmly responds. "But they were the only things I could think of. I've always been a clean-living person."

"You know, Jesus said that sin comes out of the heart of man. Our hearts are full of sin. So we don't have to murder to commit sin. Sins of pride, lust, hatred, jealousy, etc., are everyday experiences for all of us. I wanted you to look for very specific examples of things like that. Could you do so and write them down for next week?"

"Well, I'll try, but I doubt if it will be much of a list."

Problems:

1. This slice of a counseling session says nothing about Carl's presenting problem, etc. Nevertheless, it uncovers another problem that may be part of (or even basic to) such problems. What is it?

2. Do you think that Carl will produce the next time?

3. What else can the counselor do to try to help Carl?

Homework

THE ORGANIZER

Hermon tried to commit suicide. He and his wife, Lottie, are having serious marital problems.

Lottie brought the pastor a six-page, itemized and dated list of Hermon's problems. Discussion of this took the first session completely. The next week Lottie had a list of Hermon's sins that filled three more pages, while hers were written on one side of a three by five index card. The third week Lottie had made up a schedule for Hermon and was prepared to implement it.

During the fourth week, Lottie called to say that Hermon had tried again to take his life and went on for the next thirty minutes detailing all of his activities that filled the hour preceding Hermon's attempt. She then provided a list of six things to talk about when the pastor went to see him at the hospital.

Problems:

What are the problems?

1. Hermon's

2. Lottie's

3. The pastor's

Homework

Case No. 8

A SOFT ANSWER TURNS AWAY . . . JANET

Roy and Janet, members of your congregation, explained that Roy's teenage daughter Marge is the problem. She has stubbornly refused to relate positively to Janet, her new stepmother. But in this third session Janet asks: "Why are you picking on us two gals?"

Counselor: "We've been focusing on you and Marge because when you came in two weeks ago everyone agreed that the problem was between you two."

Janet: "Well, he sees the problem, but he hides behind the newspaper thinking it will go away."

Marge: "Yeah."

Counselor: "Roy, do you think this is true?"

Janet: "I know it is. There is a stone wall every time I approach him on any aspect of the problem."

Roy: "A soft answer turneth away wrath."

Janet: "See what I mean!"

Counselor: "Roy, is that answer your newspaper?"

Roy: "To be honest, yes. For the last eight or ten years I've found it much easier to absorb problems rather than to deal with them."

At this point Janet visibly relaxed for the first time since they had come to the study.

138

Problems:

1. What is happening here?

2. Is it good or bad?

3. What should the counselor do next?

Homework

LISTS

Harry and Viola came for counseling four weeks ago because communication had virtually ceased. They were both divorcees, and Harry was considerably Viola's senior. We look in on the beginning of the third session. Things so far have been developing nicely. Today the counselees are reporting on their homework assignment to choose three problems from each column and to devise biblical ways of dealing with these problems. The results of their work as they hand them to you are as follows:

Problems	Solutions
A. Harry's	
1. Overbearing	Ask rather than demand and not expect others to fetch and carry
2. Quick to anger (usually aimed at children)	Do all things in love
3. Incentive	Get up and do a thing when I think of it
B. Viola's	
4. Easily frustrated	Ask the Lord for patience
5. Very sensitive	Look at the matter from his viewpoint
6. Override husband's decisions	Be more submissive

Problems:

1. What do you think of this list?

2. Do you think that these solutions will work?

3. Has the counselor failed in any way?

Homework

PASTORAL ADVICE

Your counselee is the pastor of a nearby congregation who wants to know what his biblical course of action is in a very delicate matter of church discipline. He has come to you for advice. He explains that his church has a rule that no young couple shall be married in the church building who have conceived a child out of wedlock.

The problem is that one of his elder's daughters was married and violated this condition. He thinks that not only the couple but the parents as well perpetrated the deception that is now rather evident.

Upon finding out, the pastor confronted the young couple who confessed that it wasn't their idea to deceive the church, but her parents' idea. He then confronted the parents who denied that they had any prior knowledge of the pregnancy.

The pastor admits that he has a great deal of anger and embittered feelings toward his elder and the young couple. He wants to know what to do next, and how to handle the situation.

Problems:

1. Assuming that you would want to divide the pastor's problem into two or more parts, what would these be?

2. Does I Timothy 5:19 have any bearing upon this situation?

3. Is the pastor-counselee wrong in any ways? If so, how?

Homework

"I'M REALLY UPSET"

It is 11:25 p.m. You have been in bed for ten minutes, just on the verge of dozing off. Suddenly your phone rings. You pick up the receiver and this is what you hear: "Hello, Pastor. This is Peter—(a high school senior from your church.) I'm sorry to call so late, but I'm really upset. Linda and I just had a fight. (She is also an active member of your church.) She accused me of using her sexually—then said we should stop seeing each other. I don't think I have used her. I think I love her. I thought our relationship was going real well.

"What should I do?

"You know that both of us are Christians. You know that we want to live for the Lord. You know that we've been talking about getting married. But Linda got hysterical and accused me of being some wicked sinner. I don't understand!

"How can I patch this up?"

144

Problems:

1. What do you do next? What should be your goal for successfully completing this phone call?

2. What goals will you have for future counseling?

3. How do you propose to reach them?

4. What data do you need to proceed further?

Homework

TEEN DEPRESSION

The mother and father are very concerned about the depression and rebellion of their daughter, Millie, age 15. They do not know what is at the bottom of the problem. They think that what they need is "patience to endure this stage of rebellion" in their daughter's otherwise normal development. They are concerned about the depression, though: "Something other than rebellion is happening," dad says. You urge them to bring her in with them as soon as possible.

At the second session, Millie appears with rather obvious ambivalence and is non-responsive to the reports of her parents' observations. You confront her about her attitude and seek a commitment on her part. She refuses, won't talk, and becomes otherwise uncooperative.

Problems:

1. How do you close this session?

2. Would you schedule another? If so, with whom?

3. What may be at the roots of the girl's problem?

4. Are there any obvious areas in the parents' thinking that may need clearing up?

Homework

"WHAT'S THE USE?"

Harry was referred to your care by the parole officer who handled his case of attempted rape and attempted suicide. The officer knows that you have helped some other people that he has sent to you.

In the previous session Harry has explained the hideous tangle of his life. He is a heavy drinker, his wife left him with the children, she had been unfaithful, and he is confused about everything.

"I'm a Christian—well, I think I am. My wife is too, but she has a demon and my pastor's attempts to exorcise it have failed. I don't pray any more, because God doesn't answer. What's the use of doing anything! I just don't care."

"Harry, if you are a Christian you should care, because you know that God cares. You have done all of the work I asked you to do at our first session. That shows me that you have some concern."

"Yea, but that isn't worth much. I know that I need help, but the only reason I'm here is because of the cop that stopped me from killing myself. Nothing really matters."

Problems:

1. What do you think of Harry's profession of faith?

2. How will you deal with the attempts at rape and at suicide?

3. Do you think that he failed at both of these for the same reasons that he has been a failure before? Was he only trying to get sympathy and attention (or help)?

Homework

"I WANT TO PUNCH HER"

"Yes, this is probably the heart of it," Louise says to the counselor. "My heart *is* filled with bitterness toward Mildred."

"Now has your friend done something to elicit this reaction?" the counselor inquires.

"Well, she always butts her nose into our family affairs. We've been having some trouble with Jeff, our 17-year-old son. And we've been seeking guidance from the Lord. But Mildred seems to think that *she* has *all* the answers. She's always saying, you shouldn't do this, you shouldn't do that, you'd better do this, you'd better do that, and on and on. Sometimes I just feel like screaming. I almost want to punch her at times! She makes me *so* mad!"

"Yes, I can see that. I know that your reaction is a natural one. Most parents are defensive when they are criticized by outsiders. But you have to see something, Louise. Letting the bitterness build up is unhealthy for you. You should try to rid yourself of it. As you have already found out, it only results in increasing your frustration."

Problems:

1. This counsel lacks force. Why?

2. What is the solution to the problem?

3. How may Louise be helped to take a course of action leading to that solution?

Homework

"WE'RE READY"

"Pastor, we've talked about my problem for three weeks now. I feel that we're finally ready to get down to business and start solving my problems. How do you suggest that I begin?" Thus Karen, a less-than-happily married member of your church, begins her fourth session of counseling about her marriage to an unsaved husband. You agree with her to the extent that you think that you have finally isolated one issue that has been poisoning her relationship with her husband, planting a thorny hedge of bitterness between them. You are convinced that Bob's working schedule—one which sometimes leaves him with only one night a week at home with his family—and Karen's consequent and reactionary failure to be a disciplined wife—are together destroying possibilities for evangelizing Bob and bringing about a happy marriage.

Problems:

1. Is anything wrong here?

2. How would you proceed, intensively or extensively?

3. What is missing in this session?

Homework

"MAYBE I DON'T LOVE GOD ENOUGH"

Henry is thirty-four years old and a life-time member of your congregation. About a month and a half ago you asked him to come and see you because of periods of depression leading to total inactivity at the church over the last six months.

"I know there is something wrong. But I just don't know how to explain it. For one thing, I work too much. Unfortunately, I'm the only one who does on my shift. All the other guys just waste time," he declares.

His previous homework assignments included the task of listing sins and failures. The list is brief, abstract, and confusing. "Henry, what did you mean when you listed ambition and conscientiousness as sins? Give me some examples of what you had in mind."

"I don't know exactly what I meant. I figured that's why I don't get along at work. . . . Maybe I don't love God enough. . . ."

Problems:

1. What is one of Henry's problems?

2. How can you get to the *heart* of his difficulties?

3. Can you settle for the kind of homework that you received?

Homework

WHAT PRICE SUBMISSION?

"Hello, Pam. How was your week?" says the counselor to the high school senior as she walks into the office.

"Well, I'm sorry to say that it was a pretty disappointing week," she says. "No matter how hard I try, there seem to be too many things working against me."

"Let's have an example," responds the counselor.

"Example number one is my mother. I took your advice to listen to her and obey her instead of always arguing. But you've never met a woman like my mother. She must think that she is Attila the Hun! When I show the slightest sign of submission, she pours on the coals. You know, she made me do all of the dusting in the whole house this week. And not only that, but I missed the biggest party of the year Saturday night because I had to stay home and *babysit!* Man, this approach isn't for me. Not with a mother like mine!"

Problems:

1. What is Pam's problem?

2. How may the counselor discover and deal with it?

3. Sketch a plan of action that might meet the need.

Homework

"REAL" PROBLEMS

"Well, Bill," says the counselor at the beginning of the fourth session, "how did you do with the homework this week?"

"A little better than the week before, I think," replies the 35-year-old husband and father of three.

"Hum, I don't see any record here of starting regular family devotions," the counselor says, looking up from the papers. "What's the difficulty?"

"Well, if you really want to know," grunts Bill, I don't think that assignment has anything to do with my problems. I came in here for nervous tension and depression, right?"

"That's right, Bill, but as a Christian husband and father you have many important responsibilities. It is only when you strengthen all of the areas of your life that you will have a solid base for handling tension and depression."

"Look," says Bill as the color of his face begins to match his red tie, "I want you to help me with my problems, not cram these religious duties down my throat. I have my own kind of spiritual leadership in my home! Now let's get down to the real problems."

Problems:

1. Was the counselor or Bill correct in his contention?

2. If you think that the counselor has a point, do you think that he is correct in confronting Bill over this issue?

3. What can the counselor do next (especially consider the need to meet Bill's emotional state)?

Homework

BAD LANGUAGE

Mildred at first came alone seeking help for her marriage. In response to the homework suggested then, she was successful in bringing her husband for the third session. "Here is our homework. Jack didn't complete his lists. He only listed a few problems," says Mildred, leading off the discussion. "Why in the hell should I?" retorts Jack. "All this bastard is interested in is sticking his nose into things that are none of his business!"

"Why are you here then?" you ask.

"Because I want to get the hell rid of this religious bitch and have her leave me alone. I want you to tell this ass to give me a divorce. This religion stuff just ruined a good broad. I've got you to thank for that!"

Problems:

1. How will you handle Jack's anger and his language?

2. Is there any hope? Can hope be established?

3. What will you do next?

Homework

"I JUST CAN'T"

"Feelings of inferiority have made me sick physically and generally impotent as a person," says Gus. "I've tried to do as you said, but I just can't." At a previous session you asked Gus to seek the forgiveness of his father for several admitted offenses against him. Gus is now in his fourth session and the one assignment that has been given for the past two weeks still remains incompleted. "You 'can't,' really means you 'won't,' doesn't it?" is your reply. "No, I just can't do anything," he responds. "I'm not a quitter or anything, but I can't do *that*. I want to; I know I should and if I had more ego strength, I might be able to do so."

Problems:

1. What do you think of Gus's explanation?

2. How will you handle it?

3. Does Gus's language suggest any possible problems?

Homework

CHECK UP?

You dismissed Harry six weeks ago and set up a second check-up session after the first was canceled due to working overtime. Harry's wife called you an hour after the time of the appointment to notify you that he couldn't make it. Harry's a new Christian who has been trying to overcome drunkenness.

Harry is now sitting before you in tears confessing that he was drunk and that his problem is not solved as he had thought. "Maybe I can't stop drinking. Once a drunk always a drunk! I stayed away from all the places and people that you told me to. I even found three new ways home from work and alternate them. I guess I just don't love God enough." Harry sobbed.

"When did you get drunk and what was involved?" you inquire.

"I don't know exactly, but it began when my wife and I had an argument. She wanted to go out and I couldn't because I wanted to avoid the drinking at the club to which she wanted to go. She left any way and I started feeling bad."

Problems:

1. So far, where have you erred in counseling?

2. What correction now is necessary?

Homework

THE FINANCIAL RUIN

"I'm at the end of my rope. All of the chickens have come home to roost! I am a financial ruin. What can I do?" That was how Gary, a 26-year-old married Christian, had represented his problem at the first session. But when you quizzed him about the exact state of his finances and the precise amount of his debts and regular expenditures, he could not tell you—even roughly. For homework, he was asked to compile the necessary statistics. Now, he has come with figures that amount to the following:

Debts (not included in regular payments)
$1,000.00—personal loan
   483.00—owed to Sears
   695.00—educational loan
Regular monthly income: $1,100.00
Regular monthly obligations: $1,374.00

Problems:

1. Where do you go from here?

2. What must Gary do to solve his problem?

3. Where is his wife? Will her presence be important?

Homework

"I WORRY TOO MUCH"

Karen tells you that she is worried, and that this has led to difficulty in sleeping for the past six months. She is afraid that her marriage is falling apart. George and Karen are Christians, in their late twenties. George, a lawyer, has had to work quite a bit lately and admitted in the second session that he hasn't been able to spend much time with Karen. This, however, is a temporary situation that will end soon.

"Karen has been a faithful and conscientious helper during this time of excessive work," states George. "I love her; there is nothing wrong with our marriage!"

"He is so good to me and patient about my faults. George really is my loving—leader. My problem is that I can't sleep. I guess I just worry too much about nothing," concludes Karen.

"What specifically do you worry about?" you ask.

"I worry about my marriage. I don't want it to fail like my parents' marriage did. Everything seemed O.K. until all of a sudden, it came apart," Karen replies. "I have read Philippians 4:6, 7 on the subject of worry and I know that worry is sin, but I can't seem to stop."

Problems:

1. List all of the problems that these data seem to indicate may be present.

2. Which of these is most likely to be at the bottom of the difficulty?

3. Assuming that the problem that you have isolated is the correct one, what would you do to help Karen to overcome it?

Homework

"I COULD NEVER GO"

"Bob," says the counselor to the 19-year-old young man seated on the edge of his chair, "I think we both know that we've arrived at the heart of the matter. You laid your finger on it when you said that taking the twenty dollars from your friend's service station was the beginning of all of the other problems. But you have to *do* something about it. More talking about it here won't help now. You need to go and confess it to Tim, and pay him back."

"Yeah, I see how important it is," says the nervous red-head, "but I think I have a better idea. How about if I just send the money to him anonymously? Man, I could never look him in the face again if he found out that *I* took the money. We've been friends for a long time, and I don't want to wreck that. Talking with him about it would be about the hardest thing in the world for me. And why is it necessary any way? I think my idea is better. I'll just send the cash. What do you think?"

"Bob, you know what I think," the counselor says firmly. "It's mandatory to go to Tim *in person.*"

"No, I can't do it. I could never do it!"

Problems:

1. Do you think Bob will go?

2. Is Tim likely to break up the friendship?

3. Do you agree that Bob should see Tim? Why?

Homework

"WHERE'S THE CATHARSIS?"

"This is a serious matter, Jean," says the counselor. "This is the second week in a row that you've failed to do the homework. You haven't even begun to list your failures yet. Last week you had a plausible excuse, but here we are again, faced with the same problem. If you continue to put it off we can't make any progress. Are you really committed to change?"

"Well, I'm committed very much," says the chubby 26-year-old working girl. "But I don't see that these 'assignments' can have any part in solving my neurotic problems. I've been counseled a lot before and I never had assignments like this. Where's the catharsis in this counseling? I'm here to talk out my problems, to ventilate, not to be told what to do during the week. Aren't you going to solve my problems?"

"Jean, the most important thing that I can do to help is to point you to God's will for your life. That's what you have to conform to."

"Well, I think I'm beginning to see what you're doing. You're making a lot of value judgments, and you just want to give out pat answers, don't you? But there aren't any simple answers to complicated psychological problems. I wish you'd just listen and see how difficult my problems really are!"

Problems:

1. Does Jean have a point?

2. What is the real issue?

3. What is a likely outcome of this discussion?

4. How may the counselor ward off that eventuality?

___

Homework

"IT WAS A BAD WEEK"

"I notice you didn't attend church or Sunday School again this week," says the counselor while discussing Phyllis' homework. "Any particular reason?"

"Well, you know the problem—it's been a big struggle for me to get out with those people ever since Paul and I parted. I just hate to talk to people and to see all of those other couples who are making it," responded the 32-year-old divorcee. "Plus, it was a bad week for me. Whenever I tried to read the Bible or pray I didn't feel close to God. So even though I know He wants me to go to church and all that, when I feel so lonely and far from Him I think that it wouldn't do me any good just to sit there in church. I need to get myself straightened out before I return."

"I see," the counselor responds. "Now, before we discuss that, I have one more question. Your schedule indicates that you spent only three hours doing housework. That wasn't enough time to get all of the work done, was it?"

"Well, I guess I could have done more, but I've never been very domestic. It just doesn't come naturally to me. And this week, as I said, I just didn't feel up to it."

Problems:

1. What sinful tendency do you see in this counselee?

2. What can you do to point this out to her?

3. How would you help her to overcome it?

4. In general, what would be a good policy in dealing with such problems?

Homework

"LET'S GO FISHING"

"Well Ralph," says the counselor, "it looks like you didn't make any effort to get out with people again. And we both agreed that this is a key factor in overcoming your problems of inwardness and loneliness."

"Yes, I guess I muffed it again," says the sloppy 38-year-old single man. "But how's this for an idea? If you like to fish, maybe we could go together this Saturday."

"Ralph, even though I like to fish, this wouldn't be a good solution. I think you know that you need to develop friendships at your church. You know Christian men there."

"Sure, I know who they are, but I don't know them," says Ralph bitterly. "They're hard to get close to."

"How hard have you tried to get to know them, Ralph?"

"Well, not too hard lately, but it's tough. How do you expect me to go out and meet others if you won't even do something with me? I think if I could just get my feet wet and get to know you a bit, it would get me over a big hurdle. I enjoy talking with you. Won't you reconsider the fishing idea?"

Problems:

1. Would you be wise to agree to Ralph's request?

2. What seems to be his problem?

3. What is the best move to make at this session?

Homework

ALL THAT I REALLY WANT IS A HUSBAND

After working through the depression and other presentation problems (she was now back at work as a dental receptionist), at the outset of the fourth counseling session 24-year-old Virginia announced (as soon as she was seated), "I know that I am bitter and resentful. I am lonely and I don't like it. I know what my problem is—All that I really want is a husband!" At this she broke into sobs. Lifting her head she continued with tears streaming down her homely face, "What can I do? I am a Christian; I can't marry an unbeliever. Our church is small. There are hardly any prospects, and none ever asks me out on a date."

Problems:

1. How would you define Virginia's problem(s)?

2. What resources may you draw upon to help her meet her need?

3. If you were to suggest a timetable of activities for her, what would be the order of items on the list?

Homework

GOODBYE

"I feel much better now," said Ted as he sat down. He had come because of depression that developed when he got into difficulty with the principal of his school, and then began brooding over the difficulty rather than dealing with it. As a high school English teacher, Ted had many papers to grade. These had piled up as he continued to feel more and more depressed. You sent him back to apologize to the principal after straightening out matters with God, and to catch up on his papers. He has done both. "Just think," he continues, "After only two weeks of counseling it is all over; you have cured me! I don't know how to thank you enough. At any rate, you can assign this hour to someone else. I'm a new man!"

Problems:

1. A key counseling concept is represented by the word "WHOAH!" How does it apply in Ted's case?

2. What is needed here?

3. How will you proceed?

Homework

181

PROGRESS . . . BUT NOT LICKED

"Masturbation." The word had been spoken in Ray's first session; first by you and then by him. A senior in high school, Ray had come to you early in the summer for some straight answers and, hopefully, some helpful advice on how to break what had become a life-dominating habit.

"I want help," Ray had pleaded. "My whole thought life (not to speak of anything else) has been affected by my problem. I feel perverted and dirty—and lonely, I'm ashamed to date girls that I respect. My spiritual life is suffering. I can't go on asking God for forgiveness when I keep doing it two hours later! Every minute that I'm alone, I have to battle the urge. I'm consumed with sex; it is all that I think about. Help me; help me to stop!"

Taking Ray up on his request, you had spent the next three sessions giving him practical advice about how to break the habit. Progress was evident; he threw away his girlie magazines, stopped spending time looking at certain girls in school, etc. He now says, "I have been helped, but the problem is not licked."

Problems:

1. What more can be done?

2. Has there been a failure on your part as counselor?

3. How would you correct it (outline a concrete program)?

Homework

"THIS ISN'T LIFE"

Edna is a 57-year-old Christian widow. Her husband died five years ago, just shortly before her 16-year-old son was killed in a car accident.

Edna says that since that time she has been lonely and detached from others. She often has long periods of depression. This is magnified by the physical pain of acute arthritis.

"I have no reason to go on. Everything that gave meaning to my life is gone. I have even lost contact with God now. He seems so far away to me. I wish I could die. I wish I had died four years ago. This isn't life!"

Upon questioning you find out that Edna attends church very infrequently, and rarely reads the Word of God.

You have given her assignments calculated to bring hope, to remove the depression, and to help her start a new life, but it is now the third session and she has still done nothing that you have suggested. She has not made even the slightest attempt to change. She explains, "I just don't feel up to doing anything."

Problems:

1. What do you do now?

2. Have you possibly missed something in the past two sessions?

3. In what areas would you try to gather further information?

Homework

CHARGE—COUNTERCHARGE?

Clara comes to you stating that she has filed for divorce on the grounds of mental and bodily cruelty.

Clara returns for the third session. "I tried to get him here but he had *other* things to do," she begins. "You know what his other things are, of course. I told you all of them."

"But before I could explain that I don't want to hear such charges behind Marty's back," you respond. "This continuing hostility toward him, and the fact that though you told him you forgave him, seems to indicate that you have made little or no attempt to bury the issue and start afresh. I don't think that you understand forgiveness. You . . ."

"Forgive him! You know there is a limit. After he has beat me, and his drinking away our money maybe, but when I came home and found him in my bed with that woman, I can never bury that! He is just an immature, immoral, animalistic pig," she declares.

You tell her that it will be necessary for her to change her language about her husband and that you are here to help but not to salve her self-righteous attitude and listen to her ever-increasing charges against her husband.

"Why are you siding with him? I'm the one that belongs to this church!" She breaks into tears.

Problems:

1. What phenomena are you facing in Clara?

2. Did you err in past counseling sessions? If so, in what?

3. What will have to be done next?

Homework

DISCIPLINE

"Our church is cold and lifeless. No one is friendly. We want to know how we can go back and live with these people, because we love the church—it is so beautiful." That is the reply that you received when Mr. and Mrs. Henry responded to your inquiry about what led them to leave another Bible-teaching church in the community. You agree to help them to deal with this problem and to help them to return with the right attitude. Following three sessions, in which many bad relationships surfaced, Mr. and Mrs. Henry have returned after two weeks to report on their assignments. Mrs. Henry declares, "It was hard to apologize to that lazy, no good Mrs. Kimble, but. . . ." "Wait a minute; you have no right to speak of her that way," you reply. "But everyone knows it, and . . ." she retorts.

"Has anyone ever spoken to you about your judgmental attitude?" you ask.

There is a long pause. Mrs. Henry looks at her husband and finally she asks, "Well, are you going to tell him about that stupid church discipline or am I?"

Mr. Henry tells you that his wife was disciplined for spreading gossip over a year ago. . . . That is the real reason why they left. But till now they have withheld this information from you. "They're all a bunch of pietists," Mrs. Henry chimes in.

Problems:

1. What could the pastor have done to learn this information sooner?

2. What must he do now?

3. What must he tell the Henrys now?

Homework

"HE HAS FILED FOR DIVORCE"

"There is no hope; I thought there might be when I came last week, but I guess I was too late. Len filed for divorce two days after I came!"

"Brenda, did you tell him that you had come, that you had decided that your life had not been what it should have been as a Christian, and that you were going to work on being what God wants you to become as a woman, wife, and mother?"

"No, I didn't; I was afraid that he might be turned off, so I didn't tell him anything. Maybe I should have paid attention to you."

"Did you do your homework? May I see your list?"

"Well, I started, but after he dropped the bomb I tore it up and quit. I guess I just sat around crying and feeling sorry for myself the rest of the week."

"Well, it seems as if you have been behind all of the way; late in coming, late in telling Len, and now late in beginning to work on your own problems. While I don't want to raise any false hopes, I guess we shall now have to push ahead twice as quickly and make up for lost time. First, . . ."

Problems:

1. What do you think that this counselor will do next?

2. Isn't it too late?

3. Can you complete his final sentence?

Homework

"I TRY, BUT I CAN'T SEEM TO QUIT"

"Three times this week I have lost my temper. Even though I don't want to, I find myself blowing my stack at Mabrey every time he makes a suggestion to me. For instance, his taste is terrible and we were planning how to redecorate the powder room, and do you know what he suggested. . . . Oh! It makes me angry just to think of it! How can he be so stupid?!"

"Well, there you have it, Pastor—You can see for yourself what I've had to put up with for eight years now. I just don't see that there is much that you or anyone else can do for her. Of course the Lord could change her, but He would have to perform a miracle. Maybe she should just find another husband who doesn't irritate her so much!"

"Mabrey, . . . don't talk like that! I love you. It's true that you're stupid at times, but I love you! Help me, Pastor—you can see what a confused mess I am!"

Problems:

1. What should be the pastor's first words—to whom?

2. What does Mabrey need?

3. Assume that both are Christians, what is the best program for helping them?

Homework

"TO GO ON WOULD BE
A WASTE OF TIME . . ."

"It really would," said the pastor as he closed the folder on his desk and indicated that Matt's resistance to the gospel and lack of any willingness to read the Scriptures or discuss salvation had at last brought all progress to a screeching halt. Minimal help had been given to help Matt to iron out some difficulties with his wife, Betty, who is a member of the pastor's church. But now, attempting to help the marriage in a more fundamental way by showing the need for a Savior in the home had run into a roadblock. Matt worked willingly on trying to make up with Betty, but he balked when the pastor had indicated the need for a home in which Christ reigns. "Not for me," he said. I'm satisfied with things the way that they are. I don't need that religious stuff. Its o.k. for Betty, I don't object at all, but I don't need it. No, thanks!"

"Matt," the pastor continued, "I cannot force you to consider the claims of Christ, and I shall not pressure you. Faith must be genuine, not forced. But Betty, there are some things that I want to say to you before Matt leaves. I would like him to hear them."

Problems:

1. What do you think that the pastor is going to say to Betty?

2. Why do you suppose that he has turned to her?

3. Why does he want Matt to hear what he has to tell her?

Homework

"WHAT DO I DO NOW?"

"What will I do? I am desperate. Brad has forbidden me to attend church! I told you last week that things were getting worse all of the time. My husband is not a Christian, wants me to stay home and take care of him all of the time instead of getting involved the way that a Christian should. I appreciate the fact that you urged me to begin becoming a submissive wife, but what do I do now? When I told him that I wanted to become a submissive Christian wife he told me that I could begin by not going to the ladies group on Tuesday night, prayer meeting on Wednesday, and church twice on Sunday! Things didn't work out the way I expected! What do I do now?"

Problems:

1. O.K., it's a good question—what does she do now?

2. The pastor should have good news and bad news for her: good news

   bad news

Homework

"HE HASN'T CHANGED; HE DID IT AGAIN THIS PAST WEEK"

"What is the use? He's no better. He claims that he's trying, but there are seven days in a week; not five. How can he say that he's trying when he only remembered to open the car door five times? He'll never learn to be considerate. What's more—he said that he was going to spend more time talking to me. How many times do you suppose he tried this week?—Don't bother to guess, let me tell you—only four times!"

"But Mildred, I *am* trying. I just forget . . . and . . . and this is only the first week. I . . ."

"If you really cared, you'd show it. I don't call partial effort genuine!"

Problems:

1. How would you be likely to respond to this opening conversation?

2. Are there any questions that you might want to ask?

3. What major thrust would your remarks take toward Mildred?

toward her husband?

Homework

"A GREAT WEEK"

"Pastor, this was a great week!"

"Yeah, it was the best for months!"

"Well, I'm glad to hear that. Let's look a bit more closely at it, however, to make sure that there were real gains. Were there any arguments?"

"Not a one."

"No, there were not, he's right."

"Fran, did you clam up on Nelson this week?"

"No, I was able to overcome that problem."

"And Nelson, you didn't blow your top once?"

"Right."

"Right. See, I told you that we had done well."

"Well, let's take a look at your homework book. How did your five conferences go this week?"

"We weren't able to hold more than one this week. John was on a trip until last night. When he returned, we got right to it and laid out our work for the next week. We're all ready to go."

Problems:

1. Was this a "great week"?

2. What made the week so great?

3. What do you think of the conference that they held?

Homework

"I HAVE AN IDEA"

"I've been thinking all week, and I have an idea that I should have thought to tell you about last week. You see, I think that my depression is something that runs in the family. My mother was always getting depressed, and from time to time my sister has had problems too. I didn't try to clean my home or catch up on the washing as you told me to, since the problem must really be hereditary. It was more important for me to sit and think, you see. Besides, I just didn't feel up to doing any of the things that you suggested. I guess I'll just have to accept myself as being this way. Can you tell me, Pastor, how I can go about learning acceptance? I'm worried. It is terrible to think of being like this for the rest of my life! I don't feel like doing anything, and I really don't see much purpose or meaning in anything either. I feel so guilty for not doing my jobs as a wife and mother—the cooking, sewing, etc.—But how can I?"

Problems:

1. What do you think of the counselee's idea?

2. How would you handle her conceptually?

   motivationally?

Homework

6-WEEK CHECKUP

"Jonathan, you and Billie have really worked well over these last eight weeks. God has done many wonderful things to reverse those 'sinful trends' in your marriage of which you spoke during the first session. And frankly, today upon hearing that you have seen a permanent change in the disciplinary situation at home, I am inclined to say 'goodbye' to you. We'll schedule a final checkup session for 6 weeks to make sure that all is still going well and that we did not overlook anything. But in the meantime, over the six intervening weeks, here is what I'd like you to do."

(Below, and on the next page, write out a 6 weeks homework assignment.)

Homework

Homework (continued)

"RELIGION IS NOT MY THING"

"Did you read the Gospel of John through this week and make notes of any questions that you may have?"

"Well, Reverend, I started, but I didn't get very far. You see, all I could think about was how bad our marriage is and every time I thought about it I got discouraged and quit. Frankly, I've just about concluded that there is no hope. I came today to thank you for all of your help, but religion is not my thing and I am filing for divorce. Jeanette will never change."

"Oh! You see, Pastor, he won't try. I tell him again and again that if he would only read the Scriptures he would come to believe and we could have a Christian marriage and solve our problems and. . . ."

(At this point the counselor broke in. On the opposite page write out what he should have said and why.)

Problems:

1. What should the counselor say?

2. Justify biblically the approach taken.

Homework

"WE DIDN'T HAVE TIME"

"I see that your lists of ways to please one another are incomplete, Barry and Anne. At your first conference you were to write out seven things to do and do one each week. What happened?"

"Well, I guess we didn't do so well," Barry replies.

"How about the Code of Conduct; did you hammer that out?"

"No."

"And your schedule?"

"Unh uh."

"What got in the way of progress this week?"

"We didn't have time," Anne admits.

"Well, I can see that the need for that schedule is rather great. But until this work is done it will be impossible for us to move ahead. If you mean business for Jesus Christ, as you have claimed, you will be sorry for your poor stewardship of time this past week. So, rather than waste the rest of this hour, and become a bad steward myself, I suggest that right now. . . ."

Problems:

1. What might the counselor suggest?
   a.

   b.

2. If a., what might be the outcome?

   If b., what might be the outcome?

Homework
   (You would doubtless reassign homework not done last week.
Would you change it in any way? Would you add more?)

"HOW CAN I FORGET?"

"It's one thing to forgive him, but how can I forget? Every day I think about Joe in *her* arms, in *her* bed! I don't want to; the thoughts just come, and then—before I know it—then I am sitting there bawling like a baby. The day is ruined. I can't get back to work; I just sit there and get lower and lower. I can't help showing it either when Joe comes home."

"You can say that again, Allyson! Pastor, I tell you I don't know what I am going to do with her. I don't think that there has been a single day go by since we were here last time when she hasn't carried on this way. God forgave me when I repented, and He doesn't keep on punishing me for my sin; why should she?"

"I don't want to punish him; I just can't help think."

Problems:

1. What is Allyson's basic problem?

2. What can she do about it?

3. If you were counseling and had occasion to turn to Luke 17:3-10, how would you apply that passage to this problem?

4. Does Joe have a part to play in the solution to Allyson's problem? If so, what may he do?

Homework

"MORE THAN ONE REASON"

At the end of the fourth session Gladys became angry when her husband readily understood the point of an illustration that you made, but she didn't. You wondered at that time what effect this might have on the week, and so quickly assigned the following:

"Write down any significant events that occur this week."

Now, as you ask her to read the list of events she offers the following:

"Had my first return of depression (since counseling began) this past week.

Tues.—woke with anger over night before. Don't think Marty [her husband] really understood.

—Went back to bed with a headache [n.b., this broke schedule established week before].

—Refused Mildred's invitation to spend day shopping" [Mildred is resented by Gladys].

Here counselor broke in and discovered through probing that she refused to go because, as Gladys put it, "That would make me a hypocrite, because I'd have to smile and be nice when I really despise her." He also discovered that these thoughts continued for the rest of the day in self-pity sessions. She remembered also that she had not been thanked for taking the Sunday school class as a substitute last week. Wednesday night, looking through a drawer, she found pictures of several old girl friends. She became more depressed, getting angry over thinking how it might have been if she had pursued a career like some of them.

"The rest of the week was snafu," she wrote.

"After all," she comments, "you can see I have more than one good reason for feeling depressed."

212

Problems:

1. What problems do you see?

2. Has Gladys made an accurate connection between the week's events and her depression?

3. What does Gladys need to be told at this session?

4. If Marty is present, what will you say to him?

Homework